BURNE HOGARTH'S
LORD OF THE JUNGLE

EDGAR RICE BURROUGHS'
Tarzan.

BURNE HOGARTH'S
LORD OF THE JUNGLE

TARZAN OF THE APES
AND
JUNGLE TALES OF TARZAN

Original text by
EDGAR RICE BURROUGHS

Story adaptations by
BURNE HOGARTH and ROBERT M. HODES

Art and color work by
BURNE HOGARTH

Lettering by
BURNE HOGARTH with SKIP KOHLOFF

Foreword by
MIKE RICHARDSON

DEDICATED TO DANTON BURROUGHS

DARK HORSE BOOKS
Milwaukie, Oregon

Publisher
MIKE RICHARDSON

Collection Editor
PHILIP R. SIMON

Collection Designer
ADAM GRANO

Digital Production
CHRIS HORN and CHRISTINA McKENZIE

*Our enduring thanks to Danton Burroughs, Sandra Galfas,
and James J. Sullos Jr. at Edgar Rice Burroughs, Inc.*

Published by Dark Horse Books, a division of Dark Horse Comics, Inc.
10956 SE Main Street, Milwaukie, OR 97222
DarkHorse.com

To find a comics shop in your area, call the Comics Shop Locator Service: (888) 266-4226

First edition: June 2014
ISBN 978-1-61655-537-5

10 9 8 7 6 5 4 3 2 1
Printed in China

The Burroughs Bibliophiles is an international nonprofit literary society devoted to the life and
works of Edgar Rice Burroughs, the creator of Tarzan. The Bibliophiles publish the *Burroughs
Bulletin* journal and the *Gridley Wave* newsletter, sponsor an annual convention, and oversee
regional chapters. The *Bulletin* is the only magazine personally authorized by Burroughs. For
more information, visit BurroughsBibliophiles.com, e-mail BurroughsBibliophiles@gmail.com,
or write: Henry G. Franke III (Editor), 318 Patriot Way, Yorktown, VA 23693-4639.

TABLE OF CONTENTS

FOREWORD
BY MIKE RICHARDSON

It is no secret that the traditional newspaper business is dying. A pronounced move toward a new form of journalism fueled by social media and a multitude of mobile platforms has left the industry on the ropes and facing a grim future. There was a time, of course, when newspapers thrived and fierce competition was the order of the day. In 1940, daily circulation was estimated at 115 newspapers for every one hundred households, a figure that has since declined by about three-quarters. There is an all-but-forgotten casualty of this collapse: the Sunday comic strip. I am not referring to the tiny, four- or six-to-the-page Sunday funnies of today, but, rather, the glorious color pages of the Golden Age of the comic strip. At one time, these comics were so popular that they were actually wrapped around the *outside* of Sunday editions to increase sales. In an age in which each major city had two or more competing newspapers, a popular comic strip might be just the thing to give one paper the edge on its competition. It's easy to understand how many of the men who created these strips often became famous and even wealthy.

One such artist was Burne Hogarth. Born in Chicago on December 25, 1911, Hogarth boasted a career that included both editorial and teaching stints. He was co-founder of the School of Visual Arts and created the *Drago* strip for the Robert Hall Syndicate, but he is best remembered for the twelve years he spent illustrating the *Tarzan* Sunday strip. Following in the footsteps of his predecessor, Hal Foster, was no small task, but Hogarth managed that task with style, and he successfully (an understatement) developed an approach to comics uniquely his own. Lush jungles, fierce creatures, and "dynamic figure drawing" (his own term) combined to create one of the all-time great comic strips. Every panel meticulously planned. Every brush mark filled with purpose. His figures owed a debt to classical inspiration, but even such seemingly insignificant elements as the bend of a wrist or the position of fingers on a hand were used to enormous effect.

I first met Burne Hogarth early in 1991 when Dark Horse was just coming up on its fifth anniversary. I had created a list of great comics creators I was looking to bring to our young company, and, of course, Burne's name was near the top. I was familiar with his work, having collected the occasional reprints of his *Tarzan* Sunday strips, as well as the *Dynamic* instructional art books he authored for Watson-Guptill. As an art major in the early seventies, and a huge fan and collector of Sunday comic strips, I found these offerings to be irresistible.

I had heard that Burne was, shall we say, opinionated. While that reputation turned out to be true, it also became the basis for our friendship. Our conversations featured lively debates relating to artists, styles, books, and film, and I have to admit that I enjoyed every minute. Through it all, I continued to push Burne to create a new strip for Dark Horse. To my surprise, he pitched me *Morphos the Shapechanger*, a four-issue comics series he planned to illustrate and co-write with his friend Harry Hurwitz. I was again surprised when I saw Burne's pages . . . They were magnificent! Though in his eighties, Burne was still at the top of his game. It was then I made a decision I shall always regret. Burne was eager to see his book in print and asked to release the first completed issue even though he was just beginning work on the second. I was afraid of a long gap between issues and chose to hold to our original agreement, which called for publication upon completion of the entire series. While working on that second issue, he took time out to travel to France, where he was honored at the Angoulême Comics Festival. Burne never made it home.

Sadly, Burne Hogarth passed away on January 28, 1996, shortly after suffering a heart attack. But his tremendous legacy lives on, and we are honored to present, for the first time in decades, two of his finest works in one complete volume. Burne may be gone, but his genius remains for new generations of readers to discover herein.

—Mike Richardson, February 2014

DEDICATION

I remember a day long ago when
I was twelve. My father, with a
bundle tucked under his arm,
took me on a long street car ride
to the Art Institute of Chicago,
and there, unrolling a pile of my
drawings, sketches, and scraps he
had carefully saved, asked the
men at the desk if these were
sufficient reason to let me enroll
in the school's Saturday classes.
That's how it all started.
I give this book back to my father.
He would have been proud to see
these pages.

—Burne Hogarth, 1972

BOOK ONE

OF THE APES

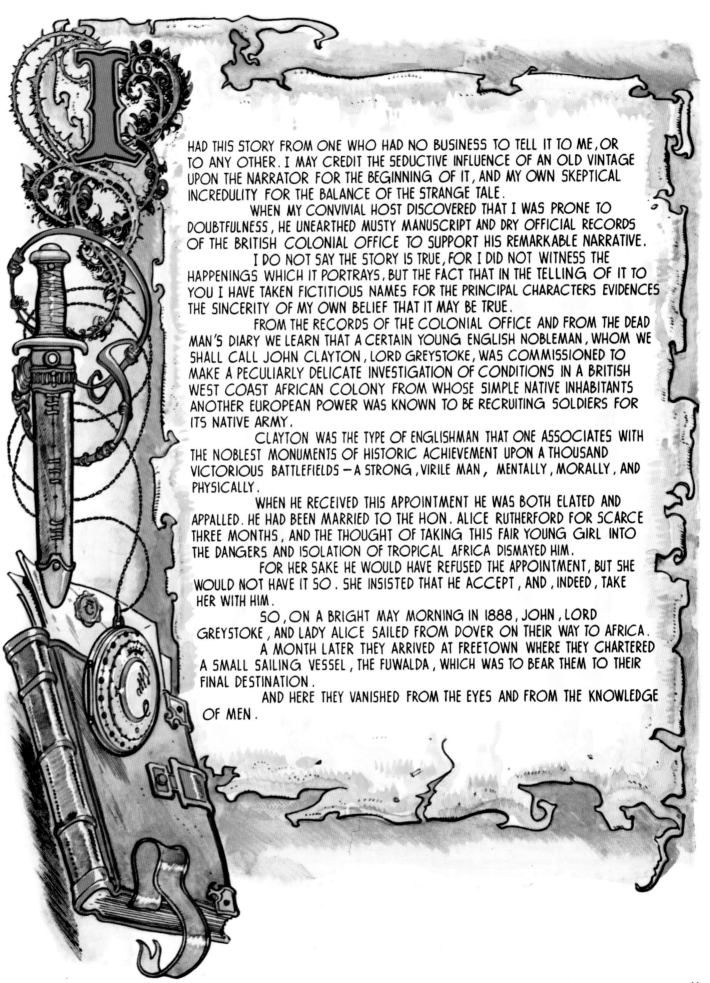

HAD THIS STORY FROM ONE WHO HAD NO BUSINESS TO TELL IT TO ME, OR TO ANY OTHER. I MAY CREDIT THE SEDUCTIVE INFLUENCE OF AN OLD VINTAGE UPON THE NARRATOR FOR THE BEGINNING OF IT, AND MY OWN SKEPTICAL INCREDULITY FOR THE BALANCE OF THE STRANGE TALE.

WHEN MY CONVIVIAL HOST DISCOVERED THAT I WAS PRONE TO DOUBTFULNESS, HE UNEARTHED MUSTY MANUSCRIPT AND DRY OFFICIAL RECORDS OF THE BRITISH COLONIAL OFFICE TO SUPPORT HIS REMARKABLE NARRATIVE.

I DO NOT SAY THE STORY IS TRUE, FOR I DID NOT WITNESS THE HAPPENINGS WHICH IT PORTRAYS, BUT THE FACT THAT IN THE TELLING OF IT TO YOU I HAVE TAKEN FICTITIOUS NAMES FOR THE PRINCIPAL CHARACTERS EVIDENCES THE SINCERITY OF MY OWN BELIEF THAT IT MAY BE TRUE.

FROM THE RECORDS OF THE COLONIAL OFFICE AND FROM THE DEAD MAN'S DIARY WE LEARN THAT A CERTAIN YOUNG ENGLISH NOBLEMAN, WHOM WE SHALL CALL JOHN CLAYTON, LORD GREYSTOKE, WAS COMMISSIONED TO MAKE A PECULIARLY DELICATE INVESTIGATION OF CONDITIONS IN A BRITISH WEST COAST AFRICAN COLONY FROM WHOSE SIMPLE NATIVE INHABITANTS ANOTHER EUROPEAN POWER WAS KNOWN TO BE RECRUITING SOLDIERS FOR ITS NATIVE ARMY.

CLAYTON WAS THE TYPE OF ENGLISHMAN THAT ONE ASSOCIATES WITH THE NOBLEST MONUMENTS OF HISTORIC ACHIEVEMENT UPON A THOUSAND VICTORIOUS BATTLEFIELDS — A STRONG, VIRILE MAN, MENTALLY, MORALLY, AND PHYSICALLY.

WHEN HE RECEIVED THIS APPOINTMENT HE WAS BOTH ELATED AND APPALLED. HE HAD BEEN MARRIED TO THE HON. ALICE RUTHERFORD FOR SCARCE THREE MONTHS, AND THE THOUGHT OF TAKING THIS FAIR YOUNG GIRL INTO THE DANGERS AND ISOLATION OF TROPICAL AFRICA DISMAYED HIM.

FOR HER SAKE HE WOULD HAVE REFUSED THE APPOINTMENT, BUT SHE WOULD NOT HAVE IT SO. SHE INSISTED THAT HE ACCEPT, AND, INDEED, TAKE HER WITH HIM.

SO, ON A BRIGHT MAY MORNING IN 1888, JOHN, LORD GREYSTOKE, AND LADY ALICE SAILED FROM DOVER ON THEIR WAY TO AFRICA.

A MONTH LATER THEY ARRIVED AT FREETOWN WHERE THEY CHARTERED A SMALL SAILING VESSEL, THE FUWALDA, WHICH WAS TO BEAR THEM TO THEIR FINAL DESTINATION.

AND HERE THEY VANISHED FROM THE EYES AND FROM THE KNOWLEDGE OF MEN.

THE FUWALDA, A BARKENTINE OF ABOUT ONE HUNDRED TONS, WAS A VESSEL OF THE TYPE OFTEN SEEN IN COASTWISE TRADE IN THE FAR SOUTHERN ATLANTIC, THEIR CREWS COMPOSED OF THE OFFSCOURINGS OF THE SEA ... UNHANGED MURDERERS AND CUTTHROATS OF EVERY RACE AND NATION. THE FUWALDA WAS NO EXCEPTION TO THE RULE. HER OFFICERS WERE BULLIES, HATING AND BEING HATED BY THEIR CREW.

THE CAPTAIN WAS A BRUTE IN HIS TREATMENT OF HIS MEN. HE KNEW BUT TWO ARGUMENTS IN HIS DEALINGS WITH THEM — THE BELAYING PIN ...

... AND REVOLVER, NOR IS IT LIKELY THAT THE MOTLEY AGGREGATION HE SIGNED WOULD HAVE UNDERSTOOD AUGHT ELSE.

SO IT WAS THAT FROM THE SECOND DAY OUT FROM FREETOWN JOHN CLAYTON AND HIS YOUNG WIFE WITNESSED SCENES UPON THE DECK OF THE FUWALDA SUCH AS THEY HAD BELIEVED WERE NEVER ENACTED OUTSIDE THE COVERS OF PRINTED STORIES OF THE SEA.

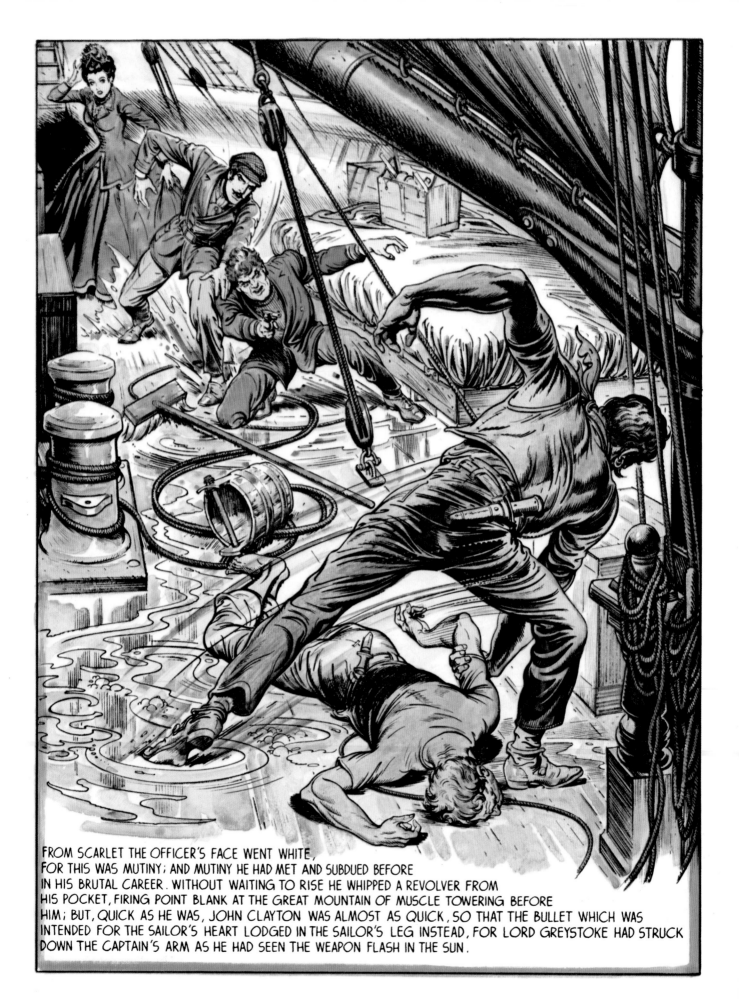

FROM SCARLET THE OFFICER'S FACE WENT WHITE,
FOR THIS WAS MUTINY; AND MUTINY HE HAD MET AND SUBDUED BEFORE
IN HIS BRUTAL CAREER. WITHOUT WAITING TO RISE HE WHIPPED A REVOLVER FROM
HIS POCKET, FIRING POINT BLANK AT THE GREAT MOUNTAIN OF MUSCLE TOWERING BEFORE
HIM; BUT, QUICK AS HE WAS, JOHN CLAYTON WAS ALMOST AS QUICK, SO THAT THE BULLET WHICH WAS
INTENDED FOR THE SAILOR'S HEART LODGED IN THE SAILOR'S LEG INSTEAD, FOR LORD GREYSTOKE HAD STRUCK
DOWN THE CAPTAIN'S ARM AS HE HAD SEEN THE WEAPON FLASH IN THE SUN.

WORDS PASSED BETWEEN CLAYTON AND THE CAPTAIN, THE FORMER MAKING IT PLAIN THAT HE WAS DISGUSTED WITH THE BRUTALITY DISPLAYED TOWARD THE CREW. THE CAPTAIN WAS ON THE POINT OF MAKING AN ANGRY REPLY, BUT, THINKING BETTER OF IT, TURNED ON HIS HEEL AND, BLACK AND SCOWLING, STRODE AFT.

BLACK MICHAEL TURNED TO CLAYTON WITH A WORD OF GRUFF THANKS. THE INCIDENT HAD ENDED...

...BUT THUS WAS FORGED THE FIRST LINK OF WHAT WAS DESTINED TO FORM A CHAIN OF CIRCUMSTANCES ENDING IN A LIFE OF ONE YET UNBORN SUCH AS HAS NEVER BEEN PARALLELED IN THE HISTORY OF MAN.

FOR SEVERAL DAYS THE CLAYTONS WERE LEFT VERY MUCH TO THEMSELVES. THIS IN ITSELF ISOLATED THEM FROM THE DAILY HAPPENINGS OF THE SHIP WHICH WERE SOON TO CULMINATE IN BLOODY TRAGEDY.

ONE MID-AFTERNOON, THE OLD SAILOR WHO HAD BEEN FELLED BY THE CAPTAIN CAME TO CLAYTON.

"MUTINY!" HE SAID, "THE CREW MEANS MUTINY AND MURDER. MARK MY WORD, IT'S COMIN', SIR."

"YOU HAVE BUT ONE DUTY, JOHN. IF YOU DO NOT WARN THE CAPTAIN YOU ARE AS MUCH A PARTY TO WHATEVER FOLLOWS AS THOUGH YOU HAD HELPED TO PLOT AND CARRY IT OUT WITH YOUR OWN HEAD AND HANDS."

"IT'S A LIE! AND IF YOU HAVE BEEN INTERFERING AGAIN WITH THE DISCIPLINE OF THIS SHIP OR MEDDLING IN AFFAIRS THAT DON'T CONCERN YOU, YOU CAN TAKE THE CONSEQUENCES, AND BE DAMNED."

"WELL, ALICE," SAID CLAYTON, AS HE REJOINED HIS WIFE, "I COULD HAVE SAVED MY BREATH. HE AND HIS BLASTED OLD SHIP MAY GO HANG, FOR AUGHT I CARE; AND UNTIL WE ARE SAFE OFF THE THING I SHALL SPEND MY ENERGIES IN LOOKING AFTER OUR OWN WELFARE."

RETURNING TO THEIR QUARTERS, THE CLAYTONS FOUND THE CABIN IN A STATE OF DISORDER. BOXES AND BAGS WERE STREWN ABOUT AND THE BEDS WERE TORN TO PIECES.

"ONLY THE REVOLVERS ARE MISSING, AND THE FACT THAT THEY WISHED FOR THEM ALONE IS THE MOST SIN-ISTER CIRCUMSTANCE OF ALL THAT HAVE TRANSPIRED SINCE WE SET FOOT ON THIS MISERABLE HULK."

THEN, AS THEY FELL TO IN AN EFFORT TO STRAIGHTEN UP THEIR CABIN, THEY NOTICED A PIECE OF PAPER BEING SLIPPED UNDER THE DOOR OF THEIR QUARTERS.

QUICKLY AND SILENTLY CLAYTON STEPPED TOWARD THE DOOR, BUT, AS HE REACHED FOR THE KNOB TO THROW IT OPEN, HIS WIFE'S HAND FELL UPON HIS WRIST.

"NO, JOHN," SHE WHISPERED. "THEY DO NOT WISH TO BE SEEN, AND SO WE CANNOT AFFORD TO SEE THEM."

"POSSIBLY OUR BEST CHANCE FOR SALVATION LIES IN MAINTAINING A NEUTRAL POSITION."

CLAYTON DROPPED HIS HAND TO HIS SIDE.

THUS THEY STOOD WATCHING THE LITTLE BIT OF WHITE PAPER UNTIL IT FINALLY REMAINED AT REST UPON THE FLOOR JUST INSIDE THE DOOR. THEN CLAYTON STOOPED AND PICKED IT UP.

KEEP YOUR MOUTHS SHUT - YOU TELL THE CAPTAIN ONE WORD ABOUT THIS AND YOU ARE DEAD!

THE NEXT MORNING, A SIGHT MET CLAYTON'S EYES WHICH CONFIRMED HIS WORST FEARS. FACING A KNOT OF OFF-ICERS WAS THE FUWALDA'S CREW, LED BY BLACK MICHAEL. AT THE FIRST VOLLEY FROM THE OFFICERS...

...THE MEN RAN FOR SHELTER, AND FROM POINTS OF VANTAGE BEHIND MASTS, WHEELHOUSE, AND CABIN THEY RETURNED THE FIRE OF THE FIVE MEN WHO REPRESENTED THE HATED AUTHORITY OF THE SHIP.

BUT AT A CRY OF COMMAND FROM BLACK MICHAEL, THE BLOOD-THIRSTY RUFFIANS, MOST OF THEM ARMED WITH BOAT HOOKS, HATCHETS AND CROWBARS, CHARGED THE OFFICERS.

IN THE INFURIATED RUSH THE CAPTAIN WAS CUT DOWN AND AN INSTANT LATER THE OTHERS WERE DOWN, DEAD OR WOUNDED FROM DOZENS OF BLOWS AND BULLET WOUNDS. SHORT AND GRISLY WAS THE WORK OF THE MUTINEERS.

NOW WITHOUT COMPASSION THEY PROCEEDED TO THROW BOTH DEAD AND DYING OVER THE SIDES OF THE VESSEL.

THROUGH IT ALL THE CLAYTONS STOOD ASIDE. NOW ONE OF THE CREW SPIED THEM. "HERE'S TWO MORE FOR THE FISHES," HE CRIED, AND RUSHED TOWARD THEM WITH UPLIFTED AX.

BUT BLACK MICHAEL WAS EVEN QUICKER.
SCARCE HAD THE FELLOW TAKEN A HALF DOZEN
STEPS WHEN HE WENT DOWN WITH A BULLET IN HIS BACK.

WITH A ROAR BLACK MICHAEL
TURNED TO THE OTHERS. "THESE HERE ARE MY FRIENDS.
THEY'RE TO BE LEFT ALONE. I'M CAPTAIN OF
THIS SHIP NOW, AN' WHAT I SAY GOES!"

ON THE FIFTH DAY FOLLOWING THE MURDER OF THE OFFICERS, LAND WAS SIGHTED. HERE, IF THE PLACE WAS HABITABLE, LORD AND LADY GREYSTOKE WERE TO BE PUT ASHORE.

BEFORE THE DARK THE BARKENTINE LAY PEACEFULLY AT ANCHOR UPON THE BOSOM OF THE STILL, MIRRORLIKE SURFACE OF THE HARBOR. THE SURROUNDING SHORES WERE BEAUTIFUL WITH SEMITROPICAL VERDURE, WHILE IN THE DISTANCE THE COUNTRY ROSE FROM THE OCEAN IN HILL AND TABLELAND, ALMOST UNIFORMLY CLOTHED BY PRIMEVAL FOREST.

AS DARKNESS SETTLED UPON THE EARTH, CLAYTON AND LADY ALICE STILL STOOD BY THE SHIP'S RAIL IN SILENT CONTEMPLATION OF THEIR FUTURE ABODE.

FROM THE DARK SHADOWS OF THE MIGHTY FOREST CAME THE WILD CALLS OF SAVAGE BEASTS — THE DEEP ROAR OF THE LION AND, OCCASIONALLY, THE SHRILL SCREAMS OF A PANTHER.

LATER IN THE EVENING BLACK MICHAEL JOINED THEM LONG ENOUGH TO INSTRUCT THEM TO MAKE THEIR PREPARATIONS FOR LANDING ON THE MORROW.

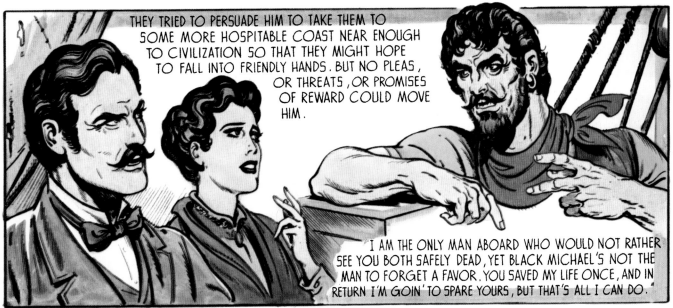

THEY TRIED TO PERSUADE HIM TO TAKE THEM TO SOME MORE HOSPITABLE COAST NEAR ENOUGH TO CIVILIZATION SO THAT THEY MIGHT HOPE TO FALL INTO FRIENDLY HANDS. BUT NO PLEAS, OR THREATS, OR PROMISES OF REWARD COULD MOVE HIM.

I AM THE ONLY MAN ABOARD WHO WOULD NOT RATHER SEE YOU BOTH SAFELY DEAD, YET BLACK MICHAEL'S NOT THE MAN TO FORGET A FAVOR. YOU SAVED MY LIFE ONCE, AND IN RETURN I'M GOIN' TO SPARE YOURS, BUT THAT'S ALL I CAN DO."

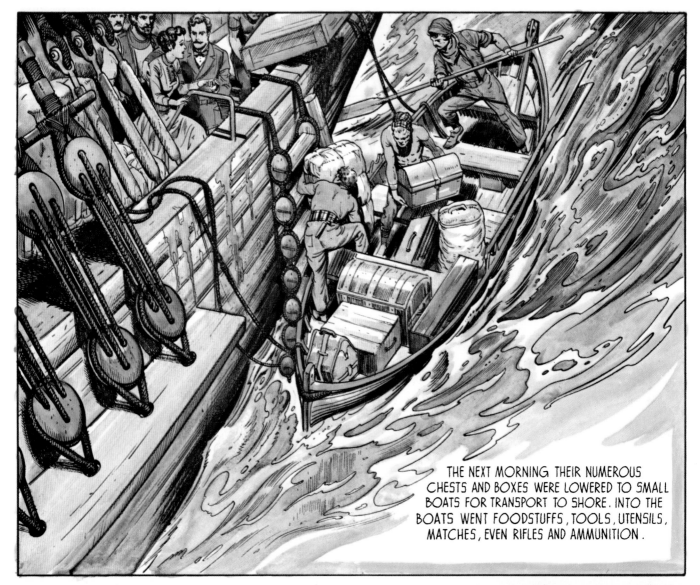

THE NEXT MORNING THEIR NUMEROUS CHESTS AND BOXES WERE LOWERED TO SMALL BOATS FOR TRANSPORT TO SHORE. INTO THE BOATS WENT FOODSTUFFS, TOOLS, UTENSILS, MATCHES, EVEN RIFLES AND AMMUNITION.

BLACK MICHAEL ACCOMPANIED THEM TO SHORE, AND WAS LAST TO LEAVE WHEN THE BOATS, THEIR CASKS FILLED WITH FRESH WATER, SHOVED OUT TO THE WAITING FUWALDA.

CLAYTON AND HIS WIFE STOOD SILENTLY WATCHING THEIR DEPARTURE WITH A FEELING OF UTTER HOPELESSNESS.

AS THEY WATCHED THE FUWALDA PASS
THROUGH THE HARBOR AND OUT OF SIGHT,
LADY ALICE BURST INTO UNCONTROLL-
ABLE SOBS. BRAVELY SHE HAD FACED
THE DANGERS OF THE MUTINY. NOW
HER NERVES GAVE WAY, AND THE
REACTION CAME.

"THERE IS ONE THING TO DO. WORK MUST BE OUR
SALVATION." "BUT JOHN, IF IT WERE ONLY YOU AND ME," SHE
SOBBED, "WE COULD ENDURE IT I KNOW; BUT . . . "

"HUNDREDS OF THOUSANDS OF YEARS AGO, OUR ANCES-
TORS OF THE DIM AND DISTANT PAST FACED THE SAME
PROBLEMS WE MUST
FACE POSSIBLY
IN THESE
SAME PRI-
MEVAL
FORESTS.

THAT WE ARE HERE TO-
DAY EVIDENCES THEIR VIC-
TORY. WHAT THEY ACCOMPLISHED, ALICE, WITH INSTRU-
MENTS AND WEAPONS OF STONE AND BONE, SURELY THAT
WE MAY ACCOMPLISH, ALSO."

CLAYTON'S FIRST THOUGHT WAS
TO ARRANGE A SLEEPING SHELTER
FOR THE NIGHT, SOMETHING
WHICH MIGHT SERVE TO PROTECT
THEM FROM PROWLING
BEASTS OF PREY.

ALL DURING THE DAY
THE FOREST ABOUT THEM
HAD BEEN FILLED WITH EXCITED
BIRDS OF BRILLIANT PLUMAGE, AND
DANCING, CHATTERING MONKEYS
WHO WATCHED THESE NEW
ARRIVALS AND THEIR WONDERFUL
NEST-BUILDING OPERATIONS
WITH EVERY MARK OF KEENEST
INTEREST AND FASCINATION.

IT WAS NOW LATE IN THE
AFTERNOON, AND THE BALANCE OF
THE DAYLIGHT HOURS WERE DEVOTED TO
THE BUILDING OF A RUDE LADDER BY
MEANS OF WHICH LADY ALICE COULD
MOUNT TO HER NEW HOME.

AND BEHIND THEM ALL, OVER THE EDGE OF A LOW RIDGE, OTHER EYES WATCHED—CLOSE-SET, WICKED EYES, GLEAMING BENEATH SHAGGY BROWS.

SUDDENLY ALICE, STRAINING HER EYES INTO THE DARKENING SHADOWS, GRASPED HER HUSBAND'S ARM. "JOHN," SHE WHISPERED. CLAYTON TURNED. "LOOK! WHAT IS IT, A MAN?"

SILHOUETTED DIMLY AGAINST THE SHADOWS BEYOND, WAS A GREAT FIGURE STANDING UPRIGHT. MOMENTARILY IT STOOD AS THOUGH LISTENING, THEN IT MELTED INTO THE SHADOWS OF THE JUNGLE.

EXHAUSTED, THEY LAY DOWN
WITHIN THEIR TINY AERIE TO TRY TO
GAIN, THROUGH SLEEP, A BRIEF RESPITE
OF FORGETFULNESS. CLAYTON LAY
FACING FRONT, RIFLE AND REVOLVERS READY AT HAND.

THEY HAD SCARCE CLOSED THEIR EYES, WHEN
THE TERRIFYING CRY OF A PANTHER RANG
OUT. THEY COULD HEAR THE BEAST
SNIFFING AND CLAWING AT THE TREES
BELOW THE PLATFORM. AT LAST
IT ROAMED AWAY, A GREAT,
HANDSOME BEAST, THE
LARGEST CLAYTON HAD
EVER SEEN.

DURING THE LONG
HOURS OF DARKNESS
THE NIGHT NOISES OF
THE JUNGLE KEPT THEIR
OVERWROUGHT NERVES ON EDGE,
AND THEIR FITFUL SNATCHES OF SLEEP
WERE LACED BY PIERCING SCREAMS
AND THE MOVING OF STEALTHY
BODIES BENEATH THEM.

MORNING FOUND THEM BUT LITTLE REFRESHED, THOUGH IT WAS WITH A FEELING OF INTENSE RELIEF THAT THEY SAW THE DAY DAWN. AS SOON AS THEY HAD MADE THEIR MEAGER BREAKFAST OF SALT PORK, COFFEE, AND BISCUIT, CLAYTON COMMENCED WORK UPON THEIR HOUSE. THE TASK WAS AN ARDUOUS ONE AND REQUIRED THE BETTER PART OF A MONTH, THOUGH HE BUILT BUT ONE SMALL ROOM. HE CONSTRUCTED HIS CABIN OF SMALL LOGS, STOPPING THE CHINKS WITH CLAY. AT ONE END HE BUILT A FIREPLACE OF SMALL STONES FROM THE BEACH.

IN THE WINDOW OPENING HE SET BRANCHES, SO WOVEN THAT THEY FORMED A SUBSTANTIAL GRATING THAT COULD WITHSTAND THE STRENGTH OF A POWERFUL ANIMAL. THE DOOR HE BUILT OF PIECES OF THE PACKING BOXES WHICH HAD HELD THEIR BELONGINGS, NAILING ONE PIECE UPON ANOTHER UNTIL HE HAD A SOLID BODY OF GREAT STRENGTH, HUNG ON TWO MASSIVE HARDWOOD HINGES. THE BUILDING OF A BED, CHAIRS, TABLE, AND SHELVES WAS A RELATIVELY EASY MATTER, SO THAT BY THE END OF THE SECOND MONTH THEY WERE WELL SETTLED, AND, BUT FOR THE CONSTANT DREAD OF ATTACK BY WILD BEASTS AND THE EVER GROW-ING LONELINESS, THEY WERE NOT UNCOMFORTABLE OR UNHAPPY.

AT NIGHT GREAT BEASTS SNARLED ABOUT THEIR TINY CABIN, BUT NOW THEY PAID LITTLE ATTENTION TO THEM, SLEEPING SOUNDLY THE WHOLE NIGHT THROUGH.

THRICE THEY HAD CAUGHT FLEETING GLIMPSES OF GREAT MAN-LIKE FIGURES, BUT NEVER AT SUFFICIENTLY CLOSE RANGE TO KNOW WHETHER THESE WERE MAN OR BRUTE.

BUT ONE AFTERNOON, WHILE CLAYTON WAS WORKING ON AN ADDITION TO THEIR CABIN, A NUMBER OF FRIGHTENED MONKEYS CAME SHRIEKING THROUGH THE TREES FROM THE DIRECTION OF THE RIDGE, AS THOUGH TO WARN HIM OF APPROACHING DANGER.

AT LAST HE SAW IT, THE THING THE MONKEYS FEARED — THE MAN-BRUTE OF WHICH THE CLAYTONS HAD CAUGHT OCCASIONAL FLEETING GLIMPSES. IT WAS APPROACHING THROUGH THE JUNGLE — A GREAT ANTHROPOID APE, AND AS IT ADVANCED, IT EMITTED DEEP GUTTERAL GROWLS AND A LOW BARKING SOUND.

CLAYTON WAS SOME DISTANCE FROM THE CABIN, ARMED ONLY WITH AN AX.

NOW THE GREAT APE CAME CRASHING DIRECTLY TOWARD HIM — AND FROM A POINT WHICH PRACTICALLY CUT OFF HIS ESCAPE. HIS CHANCES WITH THIS MONSTER WERE SMALL INDEED.

ALICE, WHAT WOULD BECOME OF ALICE? YET THERE WAS STILL A SLIGHT CHANCE OF REACHING THE CABIN. HE TURNED AND RAN, SHOUTING AN ALARM TO HIS WIFE.

LADY GREYSTOKE, HEARING THE CRY, LOOKED UP TO SEE THE APE SPRINGING WITH INCREDIBLE SWIFTNESS. WITH A LOW CRY SHE SPRANG TOWARD THE CABIN, HER SOUL FILLED WITH TERROR, FOR THE BRUTE HAD INTERCEPTED HER HUSBAND. HE STOOD AT BAY, GRASPING HIS AX, READY TO SWING SHOULD THE INFURIATED ANIMAL MAKE HIS FINAL CHARGE. "CLOSE AND BOLT THE DOOR, ALICE," HE CRIED. "I CAN FINISH THIS FELLOW OFF WITH MY AX."

BUT HE KNEW HE WAS FACING A HORRIBLE DEATH, AND SO DID SHE. THE APE, A GREAT BULL, BARED HIS FANGS IN A HORRID SNARL AND HIS EYES GLEAMED HATRED AS HE PAUSED A MOMENT BEFORE HIS PREY. OVER THE BRUTE'S SHOULDER CLAYTON SAW HIS WIFE EMERGE FROM THE CABIN, ARMED WITH A RIFLE.

HORROR AND FEAR SEIZED HIM. SHE HAD ALWAYS BEEN AFRAID OF FIREARMS, BUT NOW SHE RUSHED TOWARD THE APE FEARLESSLY LIKE A LIONESS PROTECTING ITS YOUNG.

BUT JUST THEN THE APE CHARGED AND THE MAN SWUNG THE AX WITH ALL HIS MIGHT. THE POWERFUL BRUTE TORE IT FROM CLAYTON'S GRASP.

"ALICE," SHOUTED CLAYTON, "FOR GOD'S SAKE, GO BACK!"

WITH AN UGLY SNARL, HE CLOSED UPON HIS DEFENSELESS VICTIM. BUT ERE HIS FANGS HAD REACHED THE THROAT THEY THIRSTED FOR...

...THERE WAS A SHARP REPORT AND A BULLET ENTERED THE APE'S BACK BETWEEN HIS SHOULDERS.

THROWING CLAYTON TO THE GROUND, THE BEAST TURNED UPON HIS NEW ENEMY. BEFORE SHE COULD FIRE ANOTHER BULLET, THE BRUTE LUNGED.

ALMOST AT ONCE, LORD GREYSTOKE REGAINED HIS FEET AND RUSHED FORWARD TO DRAG THE APE FROM HIS WIFE'S PROSTRATE FORM.

TO HIS SURPRISE, THE GREAT BULK ROLLED INERTLY UPON THE TURF.

THE BULLET HAD DONE ITS WORK. THE APE WAS DEAD.

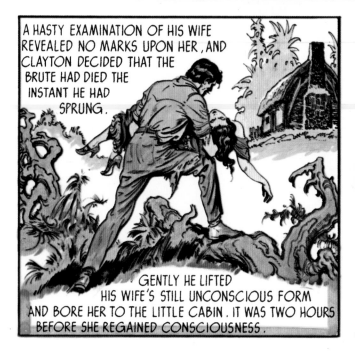

A HASTY EXAMINATION OF HIS WIFE REVEALED NO MARKS UPON HER, AND CLAYTON DECIDED THAT THE BRUTE HAD DIED THE INSTANT HE HAD SPRUNG.

GENTLY HE LIFTED HIS WIFE'S STILL UNCONSCIOUS FORM AND BORE HER TO THE LITTLE CABIN. IT WAS TWO HOURS BEFORE SHE REGAINED CONSCIOUSNESS.

BUT HER FIRST WORDS FILLED CLAYTON WITH APPREHENSION. "OH, JOHN, I'VE HAD AN AWFUL DREAM. I THOUGHT WE WEREN'T IN LONDON, BUT IN SOME AWFUL PLACE WHERE WILD BEASTS ATTACKED US." "THERE, THERE, ALICE," HE SAID. "TRY TO SLEEP AGAIN. DO NOT WORRY ABOUT BAD DREAMS."

AND THAT NIGHT A LITTLE SON WAS BORN IN THE TINY CABIN BESIDE THE PRIMEVAL FOREST WHILE A LEOPARD SCREAMED BEFORE THE DOOR AND THE DEEP NOTES OF A LION'S ROAR SOUNDED FROM BEYOND THE RIDGE.

LADY GREYSTOKE NEVER RECOVERED FROM THE SHOCK OF THE GREAT APE'S ATTACK. NOW THAT THE BABY WAS BORN, SHE NEVER VENTURED AGAIN OUTSIDE THE CABIN, NOR DID SHE EVER REALIZE SHE WAS NOT IN ENGLAND.

IN OTHER WAYS SHE WAS QUITE RATIONAL, AND THE JOY SHE TOOK IN HER LITTLE SON AND THE CONSTANT ATTENTIONS OF HER HUSBAND MADE THAT YEAR THE HAPPIEST OF HER YOUNG LIFE.

CLAYTON HAD LONG SINCE GIVEN UP ANY HOPE OF RESCUE, SO THAT WHILE HE SUFFERED TERRIBLY TO SEE HER SO, YET HE WAS ALMOST GLAD SHE COULD NOT UNDERSTAND.

WITH UNREMITTING ZEAL, HE WORKED TO BEAUTIFY AND STRENGTHEN THE CABIN.

DURING THE YEAR THAT
FOLLOWED, CLAYTON WAS
SEVERAL TIMES ATTACKED BY
THE GREAT APES WHICH
NOW SEEMED TO CONTINUALLY
INFEST THE VICINITY OF THE
CABIN ; BUT AS HE NEVER AGAIN
VENTURED OUTSIDE WITHOUT
BOTH RIFLE AND REVOLVERS , HE
HAD LITTLE FEAR OF THE HUGE BEASTS.

IN HIS LEISURE CLAYTON
READ ALOUD TO HIS WIFE FROM THE STORE OF BOOKS
HE HAD BROUGHT. AMONG THESE WERE PICTURE BOOKS,
PRIMERS, READERS FOR CHILDREN SINCE THEY HAD KNOWN
THEIR CHILD WOULD BE OLD ENOUGH FOR SUCH BEFORE
THEY MIGHT HOPE TO RETURN TO ENGLAND.

AT OTHER TIMES, CLAYTON
WROTE IN HIS DIARY, WHICH
HE HAD ALWAYS BEEN
ACCUSTOMED TO KEEP
IN FRENCH ...

... AND IN WHICH HE RECORDED
THE DETAILS OF THEIR STRANGE LIFE. THIS BOOK HE
KEPT LOCKED IN A LITTLE METAL BOX.

A YEAR FROM THE DAY HER LITTLE
SON WAS BORN, LADY ALICE PASSED QUIETLY
AWAY IN THE NIGHT. SO PEACEFUL WAS HER END THAT
IT WAS HOURS BEFORE CLAYTON COULD AWAKE TO
A REALIZATION THAT HIS WIFE WAS DEAD.

THE HORROR OF THE SITUATION
CAME TO HIM VERY SLOWLY, AND IT
IS DOUBTFUL THAT HE EVER FULLY
REALIZED THE ENORMITY OF HIS SORROW
AND THE FEARFUL RESPONSIBILITY THAT HAD
DEVOLVED UPON HIM WITH THE CARE OF THAT
WEE THING, HIS SON, STILL A NURSING BABE.

THE LAST ENTRY IN HIS DIARY WAS MADE THE
MORNING FOLLOWING HER DEATH, AND THERE HE RECITES THE SAD DETAILS IN A MATTER-
OF-FACT WAY THAT ADDS TO THE PATHOS OF IT; FOR IT BREATHES A TIRED APATHY BORN OF LONG SORROW
AND HOPELESSNESS, WHICH EVEN THIS CRUEL BLOW COULD SCARCELY AWAKE TO FURTHER SUFFERING: "MY LITTLE
SON IS CRYING FOR NOURISHMENT—O, ALICE, ALICE, WHAT SHALL I DO?" AND AS JOHN CLAYTON WROTE THESE
LAST WORDS, HE DROPPED HIS HEAD WEARILY TO HIS OUTSTRETCHED ARMS UPON THE TABLE HE HAD BUILT FOR HER
WHO LAY COLD AND STILL IN THE BED BESIDE HIM.

FOR A LONG TIME
NO SOUND BROKE THE
DEATHLIKE STILLNESS OF THE
JUNGLE MIDDAY SAVE THE PITEOUS
WAILING OF THE TINY MAN-CHILD.

KERCHAK WAS A HUGE KING APE, WEIGHING PERHAPS THREE HUNDRED AND FIFTY POUNDS. HIS FOREHEAD WAS EXTREMELY LOW AND RECEDING, HIS EYES BLOODSHOT, SMALL AND CLOSE-SET TO HIS COARSE, FLAT NOSE; HIS EARS LARGE AND THIN, BUT SMALLER THAN MOST OF HIS KIND. HIS AWFUL TEMPER AND HIS MIGHTY STRENGTH MADE HIM SUPREME AMONG THE LITTLE TRIBE INTO WHICH HE HAD BEEN BORN SOME TWENTY YEARS BEFORE.

NOW THAT HE WAS IN HIS PRIME, THERE WAS NO SIMIAN IN ALL THE MIGHTY FOREST THROUGH WHICH HE ROVED THAT DARED CONTEST HIS RIGHT TO RULE.

OLD TANTOR, THE ELEPHANT, ALONE OF ALL THE WILD SAVAGE LIFE, FEARED HIM NOT—AND HE ALONE DID KERCHAK FEAR.

THE TRIBE OF ANTHROPOIDS OVER WHICH KERCHAK RULED WITH AN IRON HAND AND BARED FANGS, NUMBERED SOME SIX OR EIGHT FAMILIES, EACH FAMILY CONSISTING OF AN ADULT MALE WITH HIS WIVES AND THEIR YOUNG, NUMBERING IN ALL SOME SIXTY OR SEVENTY APES.

KALA WAS THE YOUNGEST WIFE OF A MALE NAMED TUBLAT, MEANING BROKEN NOSE, AND HER CHILD WAS HER FIRST, FOR SHE WAS BUT NINE OR TEN YEARS OLD.

NOTWITHSTANDING HER YOUTH, SHE WAS LARGE AND POWERFUL—A SPLENDID, CLEAN-LIMBED ANIMAL, WITH A ROUND, HIGH FOREHEAD WHICH DENOTED MORE INTELLIGENCE THAN MOST OF HER KIND POSSESSED. SO, ALSO, SHE HAD A GREATER CAPACITY FOR MOTHER LOVE AND MOTHER SORROW.

NOW, IN THE FOREST OF THE TABLELAND A MILE BACK FROM THE OCEAN, KERCHAK WAS ON A RAMPAGE OF RAGE AMONG HIS PEOPLE. THE YOUNGER AND LIGHTER MEMBERS OF HIS TRIBE SCAMPERED TO THE HIGHER BRANCHES OF THE GREAT TREES TO ESCAPE HIS WRATH, RISKING THEIR LIVES UPON BRANCHES THAT SCARCE SUPPORTED THEIR WEIGHT RATHER THAN FACE OLD KERCHAK IN ONE OF HIS FITS OF UNCONTROLLED ANGER. THE OTHER MALES SCATTERED...

...BUT NOT BEFORE THE INFURIATED BRUTE HAD FELT THE VERTEBRA OF ONE SNAP BETWEEN HIS GREAT, FOAMING JAWS.

THEN HE SPIED KALA, WHO, RETURNING FROM A SEARCH FOR FOOD WITH HER YOUNG BABE, WAS IGNORANT OF KERCHAK'S TEMPER UNTIL SUDDENLY SHRILL WARNINGS CAUSED HER TO SCAMPER MADLY FOR SAFETY.

BUT KERCHAK WAS CLOSE UPON HER, SO CLOSE THAT HE HAD ALMOST GRASPED HER ANKLE HAD SHE NOT MADE A FURIOUS LEAP FAR INTO SPACE FROM ONE TREE TO ANOTHER.

SHE MADE THE LEAP SUCCESSFULLY, BUT AS SHE GRASPED THE LIMB OF THE FURTHER TREE, THE SUDDEN JAR LOOSENED THE HOLD OF THE TINY BABE WHERE IT CLUNG FRANTICALLY TO HER NECK, AND SHE SAW THE LITTLE THING HURLED, TURNING AND TWISTING, TO THE GROUND THIRTY FEET BELOW.

WITH A LOW CRY OF DISMAY,
KALA RUSHED HEADLONG TO ITS SIDE,
THOUGHTLESS NOW OF THE DANGER FROM KERCHAK;
BUT WHEN SHE GATHERED THE WEE, MANGLED FORM TO HER
BOSOM LIFE HAD LEFT IT. WITH LOW MOANS, SHE SAT CUDDLING THE BODY
TO HER; NOR DID KERCHAK ATTEMPT TO MOLEST HER. WITH THE DEATH OF THE BABE,
HIS FIT OF DEMONIACAL RAGE PASSED AS SUDDENLY AS IT HAD SEIZED HIM.

WHEN THE TRIBE SAW THAT KERCHAK'S RAGE HAD
CEASED, THEY CAME SLOWLY DOWN FROM THEIR AR-
BOREAL RETREATS AND PURSUED AGAIN THE VARIOUS
OCCUPATIONS WHICH HE HAD INTERRUPTED. THEY HAD
PASSED AN HOUR OR SO THUS WHEN KERCHAK CALLED
THEM TOGETHER AND, WITH A WORD OF COMMAND TO
THEM TO FOLLOW HIM, SET OFF TOWARD THE SEA.

ALL THE WAY, KALA CARRIED HER LITTLE DEAD BABY CLOSE TO HER BREAST
SHORTLY AFTER NOON, THEY REACHED THE BEACH WHERE LAY THE TINY COTTAGE
WHICH WAS KERCHAK'S GOAL KERCHAK HAD MADE UP HIS MIND TO EXPLORE THE INTERIOR OF THAT
MYSTERIOUS DEN, AND HE WANTED THE LITTLE BLACK STICK THAT MADE A LOUD NOISE AND BROUGHT DEATH
FROM THE HANDS OF THE STRANGE WHITE APE.

TODAY THERE WAS NO SIGN
OF THE MAN ABOUT. SLOWLY,
CAUTIOUSLY, THEY CREPT TOWARD
THE LITTLE CABIN, THE DOOR
WAS OPEN.

ON THEY CAME. KERCHAK, AND BEHIND HIM TWO MALES, THEN KALA, STRAINING THE LITTLE DEAD FORM TO HER BREAST.

KERCHAK HIMSELF SLUNK STEALTHILY TO THE VERY DOOR AND PEERED WITHIN.

THE SIGHT THAT MET CLAYTON'S EYES FROZE HIM WITH HORROR.

INSIDE THE DEN THEY SAW THE STRANGE WHITE APE LYING HALF ACROSS A TABLE, HIS HEAD BURIED IN HIS ARMS; AND ON THE BED LAY A FIGURE COVERED BY A SAIL-CLOTH, WHILE FROM A TINY RUSTIC CRADLE CAME THE PLAINTIVE WAILING OF A BABE. NOISELESSLY THEY ENTERED.

KERCHAK STRUCK, AND
WHEN HE RELEASED THE LIMP
FORM WHICH HAD BEEN
LORD GREYSTOKE HE
TURNED HIS ATTENTION TO
THE CRADLE.

BUT KALA WAS THERE BEFORE HIM. BEFORE HE COULD
GRASP THE CHILD, SHE SNATCHED THE LIVE BABY OF LADY
ALICE, DROPPED THE DEAD BABY OF HER OWN IN THE CRADLE,
AND BOLTED THROUGH THE DOOR.

HIGH AMONG THE TREES SHE HUGGED THE
SHRIEKING INFANT TO HER BOSOM, AND SOON THE IN-
STINCT THAT WAS DOMINANT IN THIS FIERCE FEMALE REACHED
OUT TO THE TINY MAN-CHILD AND HE BECAME
QUIET. THEN HUNGER CLOSED THE GAP BETWEEN THEM AND
THE SON OF AN ENGLISH LORD AND LADY NURSED
AT THE BREAST OF KALA, THE GREAT APE.

SATISFIED THE TWO CLAYTONS WERE DEAD, KERCHAK PAUSED BEFORE THE DEATH-DEALING THUNDERSTICK ON THE WALL. CAUTIOUSLY HE REGARDED IT.

NOW IT WAS IN HIS HAND. HE FELT OF IT FROM END TO END, PEERED DOWN ITS MIDDLE, FINGERED THE BREECH, AND FINALLY THE TRIGGER.

THERE WAS A DEAFENING ROAR AND THE APES FELL OVER ONE ANOTHER IN THEIR WILD ANXIETY TO ESCAPE.

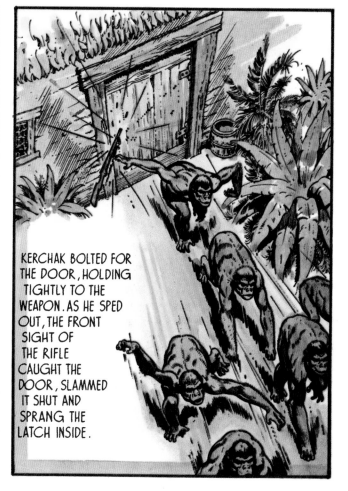

KERCHAK BOLTED FOR THE DOOR, HOLDING TIGHTLY TO THE WEAPON. AS HE SPED OUT, THE FRONT SIGHT OF THE RIFLE CAUGHT THE DOOR, SLAMMED IT SHUT AND SPRANG THE LATCH INSIDE.

IT WAS AN HOUR BEFORE
THE APES COULD AGAIN
BRING THEMSELVES TO
APPROACH THE CABIN,
AND WHEN THEY FINALLY DID SO,
THEY FOUND THAT THE DOOR WAS
SO SECURELY FASTENED THAT THEY
COULD NOT FORCE IT. THE CLEVERLY
CONSTRUCTED LATCH WHICH CLAYTON HAD MADE
HAD SPRUNG AS KERCHAK PASSED OUT; NOR COULD THE APES
FIND MEANS OF INGRESS THROUGH THE HEAVILY BARRED WINDOWS.

AFTER ROAMING ABOUT THE VICINITY FOR A SHORT TIME, THEY STARTED BACK
FOR THE DEEPER FORESTS AND THE HIGHER LAND FROM WHENCE THEY HAD COME.

KALA HAD NOT ONCE COME TO
EARTH WITH HER LITTLE ADOPTED BABE, BUT
NOW KERCHAK CALLED TO HER TO DESCEND,
AND AS THERE WAS NO NOTE OF ANGER IN HIS
VOICE SHE JOINED THE OTHERS ON THE
HOMEWARD MARCH.

ON THE JOURNEY, SHE CLUNG DESPERATELY TO THE NEW BABE. SHE HAD SEEN ONE CHILD FALL TO A TERRIBLE DEATH AND
SHE WOULD TAKE NO CHANCES WITH THIS ONE. THOSE OF THE APES WHO ATTEMPTED TO EXAMINE KALA'S STRANGE BABY
WERE REPULSED WITH BARED FANGS AND LOW GROWLS, ACCOMPANIED BY WORDS OF WARNING FROM KALA.

TENDERLY KALA NURSED HER LITTLE WAIF,
WONDERING SILENTLY WHY IT DID NOT GAIN
STRENGTH AND AGILITY AS DID THE LITTLE APES
OF OTHER MOTHERS. IT WAS NEARLY A YEAR
FROM THE TIME THE LITTLE FELLOW CAME INTO
HER POSSESSION BEFORE HE WOULD WALK
ALONE, AND AS FOR CLIMBING — MY, BUT HOW
STUPID HE WAS!

KALA SOMETIMES TALKED WITH THE OLDER
FEMALES ABOUT HER YOUNG HOPEFUL, BUT NONE
OF THEM COULD UNDERSTAND HOW A CHILD
COULD BE SO SLOW AND BACKWARD IN
LEARNING TO CARE FOR ITSELF. WHY, IT COULD
NOT EVEN FIND FOOD ALONE, AND MORE THAN
TWELVE MOONS HAD PASSED SINCE KALA HAD
COME UPON IT.

HAD THEY KNOWN THAT THE
CHILD HAD SEEN THIRTEEN MOONS
BEFORE IT CAME INTO KALA'S
POSSESSION, THEY WOULD HAVE
CONSIDERED ITS CASE AS
ABSOLUTELY HOPELESS, FOR THE
LITTLE APES OF THEIR OWN TRIBE
WERE AS FAR ADVANCED IN TWO
OR THREE MOONS AS WAS THIS
LITTLE STRANGER AFTER
TWENTY-FIVE.

TUBLAT, KALA'S HUSBAND, WAS SORELY VEXED, AND BUT FOR THE FEMALE'S CAREFUL WATCHING, WOULD HAVE
PUT THE CHILD OUT OF THE WAY. "HE WILL NEVER BE A GREAT APE," HE ARGUED. "ALWAYS WILL YOU HAVE TO CARRY
HIM AND PROTECT HIM. WHAT GOOD WILL HE BE TO THE TRIBE? NONE; ONLY A BURDEN. LET US LEAVE HIM
QUIETLY SLEEPING AMONG THE TALL GRASSES, THAT YOU MAY BEAR OTHER AND STRONGER APES TO GUARD
US IN OUR OLD AGE." "NEVER, BROKEN NOSE," REPLIED KALA. "IF I MUST CARRY HIM FOREVER, SO BE IT."

AND THEN TUBLAT WENT TO KERCHAK TO URGE HIM TO USE HIS AUTHORITY WITH KALA AND FORCE HER TO
GIVE UP LITTLE TARZAN, WHICH WAS THE NAME THEY HAD GIVEN TO THE TINY LORD GREYSTOKE, AND WHICH MEANT
"WHITE SKIN." BUT WHEN KERCHAK SPOKE TO HER ABOUT IT, KALA THREATENED TO RUN AWAY FROM THE TRIBE IF
THEY DID NOT LEAVE HER IN PEACE WITH THE CHILD.

AS TARZAN GREW, HE MADE RAPID STRIDES, SO THAT BY THE TIME HE WAS TEN YEARS OLD HE WAS AN EXCELLENT CLIMBER AND COULD DO MANY WONDERFUL THINGS WHICH WERE BEYOND THE POWERS OF HIS BROTHERS AND SISTERS.

IN MANY WAYS DID HE DIFFER FROM THEM, AND THEY OFTEN MARVELED AT HIS SUPERIOR CUNNING, BUT IN STRENGTH AND SIZE HE WAS DEFICIENT; FOR AT TEN THE GREAT ANTHROPOIDS WERE FULLY GROWN, SOME OF THEM TOWERING OVER SIX FEET IN HEIGHT... WHILE TARZAN WAS STILL BUT A HALF GROWN BOY.

YET SUCH A BOY! FROM EARLY INFANCY HE HAD USED HIS HANDS TO SWING FROM BRANCH TO BRANCH AFTER THE MANNER OF HIS GIANT MOTHER, AND AS HE GREW OLDER HE SPENT HOUR UPON HOUR DAILY SPEEDING THROUGH THE TREE TOPS. HE COULD SPRING TWENTY FEET ACROSS SPACE AT THE DIZZY HEIGHTS OF THE FOREST TOP AND GRASP WITH UNERRING PRECISION A LIMB WAVING WILDLY IN THE PATH OF AN APPROACHING TORNADO.

HE COULD DROP TWENTY FEET AT A STRETCH FROM LIMB TO LIMB IN RAPID DESCENT TO THE GROUND...

...OR HE COULD GAIN THE UTMOST PINNACLE OF THE LOFTIEST TROPICAL GIANT WITH THE EASE AND SWIFTNESS OF A SQUIRREL. THOUGH BUT TEN YEARS OLD, HE WAS FULLY AS STRONG AS THE AVERAGE MAN OF THIRTY, AND FAR MORE AGILE THAN THE MOST PRACTICED ATHLETE EVER BECOMES. AND DAY BY DAY HIS STRENGTH WAS INCREASING. HIS LIFE AMONG THESE FIERCE APES WAS HAPPY; FOR HIS RECOLLECTION HELD NO OTHER LIFE...

...NOR DID HE KNOW THAT THERE EXISTED IN THE UNIVERSE AUGHT ELSE THAN HIS LITTLE FOREST AND THE WILD JUNGLE ANIMALS WITH WHICH HE WAS FAMILIAR.

HE WAS NEARLY TEN WHEN HE REALIZED THAT A GREAT DIFFERENCE EXISTED BETWEEN HIMSELF AND HIS FELLOWS. HIS LITTLE BODY, BURNED BROWN BY EXPOSURE, SUDDENLY CAUSED HIM FEELINGS OF INTENSE SHAME, FOR HE REALIZED THAT IT WAS ENTIRELY HAIRLESS, LIKE SOME LOW SNAKE OR OTHER REPTILE.

HE ATTEMPTED TO OBVIATE THIS BY PLASTERING HIMSELF FROM HEAD TO FOOT WITH MUD, BUT THIS DRIED AND FELL OFF. BESIDES, IT FELT SO UNCOMFORTABLE THAT HE QUICKLY DECIDED THAT HE PREFERRED THE SHAME TO THE DISCOMFORT.

IN THE HIGHER LAND WHICH HIS TRIBE FREQUENTED WAS A LITTLE LAKE, AND IT WAS HERE THAT TARZAN FIRST SAW HIS FACE IN THE CLEAR, STILL WATERS OF ITS BOSOM.

IT WAS ON A SULTRY DAY OF THE DRY SEASON THAT HE AND ONE OF HIS COUSINS HAD GONE DOWN TO THE BANK TO DRINK. AS THEY LEANED OVER, BOTH LITTLE FACES WERE MIRRORED ON THE PLACID POOL: THE FIERCE AND TERRIBLE FEATURES OF THE APE BESIDE THOSE OF THE ARISTOCRATIC SCION OF AN OLD ENGLISH HOUSE. TARZAN WAS APPALLED. IT HAD BEEN BAD ENOUGH TO BE HAIRLESS, BUT TO OWN SUCH A COUNTENANCE! HE WONDERED THAT THE OTHER APES COULD LOOK AT HIM AT ALL. THAT TINY SLIT OF A MOUTH AND THOSE PUNY WHITE TEETH! HOW THEY LOOKED BESIDE THE MIGHTY LIPS AND POWERFUL FANGS OF HIS MORE FORTUNATE BROTHERS! AND THE LITTLE PINCHED NOSE OF HIS; SO THIN WAS IT THAT IT LOOKED HALF STARVED.

HE TURNED RED AS HE COMPARED IT WITH THE BEAUTIFUL BROAD NOSTRILS OF HIS COMPANION. SUCH A GENEROUS NOSE! WHY IT SPREAD HALF ACROSS HIS FACE! IT CERTAINLY MUST BE FINE TO BE SO HANDSOME, THOUGHT POOR LITTLE TARZAN. BUT WHEN HE SAW HIS OWN EYES; AH, THAT WAS THE FINAL BLOW — A BROWN SPOT, A GRAY CIRCLE, AND THEN BLANK WHITENESS! FRIGHTFUL! NOT EVEN THE SNAKES HAD SUCH HIDEOUS EYES AS HE.

SO INTENT WAS HE
UPON THIS PERSONAL
APPRAISEMENT OF HIS
FEATURES THAT HE DID NOT
HEAR THE PARTING OF THE TALL
GRASS BEHIND HIM AS A GREAT
BODY PUSHED ITSELF STEALTHILY
THROUGH THE JUNGLE; NOR DID HIS
COMPANION, THE APE, HEAR EITHER, FOR
HE WAS DRINKING AND THE NOISE OF HIS
SUCKING LIPS AND GURGLES OF SATISFACTION
DROWNED THE QUIET APPROACH OF THE INTRUDER.

NOT THIRTY PACES BEHIND THE TWO SHE CROUCHED—
SABOR, THE LIONESS—LASHING HER TAIL. CAUTIOUSLY SHE
MOVED A GREAT PADDED PAW FORWARD, NOISELESSLY PLACING
IT BEFORE SHE LIFTED THE NEXT. THUS SHE ADVANCED, HER BELLY
LOW, ALMOST TOUCHING THE SURFACE OF THE GROUND—A
GREAT CAT PREPARING TO SPRING UPON ITS PREY.

NOW SHE WAS WITHIN TEN FEET OF THE TWO UNSUSPECTING LITTLE PLAYFELLOWS — CAREFULLY SHE DREW HER HIND FEET WELL UP BENEATH HER BODY, THE GREAT MUSCLES ROLLING UNDER THE BEAUTIFUL SKIN.

SO LOW WAS SHE CROUCHING NOW THAT SHE SEEMED FLATTENED TO THE EARTH EXCEPT FOR THE UPWARD BEND OF THE GLOSSY BACK AS IT GATHERED FOR THE SPRING.

NO LONGER THE TAIL LASHED — QUIET AND STRAIGHT BEHIND HER IT LAY. AN INSTANT SHE PAUSED THUS AS THOUGH TURNED TO STONE...

...AND THEN, WITH AN AWFUL SCREAM, SHE SPRANG.

HER SCREAM WAS NOT A WARNING . IT
PRODUCED A PARALYSIS OF TERROR AS
THE LITTLE APE CROUCHED AND FROZE—
AND THAT WAS HIS UNDOING . NOT SO, HOWEVER,
WITH TARZAN, THE MAN-CHILD . HIS LIFE AMIDST THE
DANGERS OF THE JUNGLE HAD TAUGHT HIM TO MEET
EMERGENCIES WITH SELF-CONFIDENCE , AND HIS
HIGHER INTELLIGENCE RESULTED IN A QUICKNESS OF
MENTAL ACTION FAR BEYOND THE POWERS OF THE APES.
THE CRY OF SABOR GALVANIZED HIM INTO INSTANT
ACTION . INTO THE DEEP WATERS OF THE LAKE HE PLUNGED ...

... AN EVIL HARDLY LESS THAN SABOR'S FANGS—FOR HE COULD NOT SWIM . RAPIDLY HE MOVED HIS HANDS AND FEET . BY
CHANCE HE FELL INTO A STROKE A DOG USES . IN A FEW SECONDS HIS NOSE WAS ABOVE WATER .

THE LIONESS WAS INTENTLY WATCHING TARZAN, EVIDENTLY EXPECTING HIM TO RETURN TO SHORE, BUT THIS THE BOY HAD NO INTENTION OF DOING. INSTEAD HE RAISED HIS VOICE IN THE CALL OF DISTRESS COMMON TO HIS TRIBE.

ALMOST IMMEDIATELY FORTY OR MORE GREAT APES SWUNG TOWARD THE SCENE.

WITH A SNARL OF HATRED THE LIONESS VANISHED. TARZAN NOW SWAM TO SHORE EXHILARATED BY THE EXPERIENCE AND THE KNOWLEDGE OF HIS NEW-FOUND SKILL. AND EVER AFTER HE LOST NO OPPORTUNITY TO TAKE A DAILY PLUNGE IN LAKE OR STREAM OR OCEAN WHEN IT WAS POSSIBLE TO DO SO.

FOR A LONG TIME KALA COULD NOT ACCUSTOM HERSELF TO THE SIGHT; FOR THOUGH HER PEOPLE COULD SWIM WHEN FORCED TO IT, THEY DID NOT LIKE TO ENTER WATER, AND NEVER DID SO VOLUNTARILY.

THE ADVENTURE WITH THE LIONESS GAVE TARZAN FOOD FOR PLEASURABLE MEMORIES, FOR IT WAS SUCH AFFAIRS WHICH BROKE THE MONOTONY OF HIS DAILY LIFE — OTHERWISE BUT A DULL ROUND OF SEARCHING FOR FOOD, EATING, AND SLEEPING. THE TRIBE TO WHICH HE BELONGED ROAMED A TRACT EXTENDING, ROUGHLY, TWENTY-FIVE MILES ALONG THE SEACOAST AND SOME FIFTY MILES INLAND. THIS THEY TRAVERSED ALMOST CONTINUALLY, OCCASIONALLY REMAINING FOR MONTHS IN ONE LOCALITY; BUT AS THEY MOVED THROUGH THE TREES WITH GREAT SPEED, THEY OFTEN COVERED THE TERRITORY IN A VERY FEW DAYS.

MUCH DEPENDED UPON FOOD SUPPLY, CLIMATIC CONDITIONS, AND THE PREVALENCE OF ANIMALS OF THE MORE DANGEROUS SPECIES; THOUGH KERCHAK OFTEN LED THEM ON LONG MARCHES FOR NO OTHER REASON THAN THAT HE HAD TIRED OF REMAINING IN THE SAME PLACE.

AT NIGHT THEY SLEPT WHERE DARKNESS OVERTOOK THEM, LYING UPON THE GROUND, AND SOMETIMES COVERING THEIR HEADS, AND MORE SELDOM THEIR BODIES, WITH THE GREAT LEAVES OF THE ELEPHANT'S EAR. TWO OR THREE MIGHT LIE CUDDLED IN EACH OTHER'S ARMS FOR ADDITIONAL WARMTH IF THE NIGHT WERE CHILL, AND THUS TARZAN HAD SLEPT IN KALA'S ARMS NIGHTLY FOR ALL THESE YEARS.

THAT THE HUGE, FIERCE BRUTE LOVED THIS CHILD OF ANOTHER RACE IS BEYOND QUESTION, AND HE, TOO, GAVE TO THE GREAT, HAIRY BEAST ALL THE AFFECTION THAT WOULD HAVE BELONGED TO HIS FAIR YOUNG MOTHER HAD SHE LIVED. WHEN HE WAS DISOBEDIENT SHE CUFFED HIM, IT IS TRUE, BUT SHE WAS NEVER CRUEL TO HIM, AND WAS MORE OFTEN CARESSING HIM THAN CHASTISING HIM.

TUBLAT, HER HUSBAND, ALWAYS HATED TARZAN, AND ON SEVERAL OCCASIONS HAD COME NEAR ENDING HIS YOUTHFUL CAREER.

TARZAN ON HIS PART NEVER LOST AN OPPORTUNITY TO SHOW THAT HE FULLY RECIPROCATED HIS FOSTER FATHER'S SENTIMENTS, AND WHENEVER HE COULD SAFELY ANNOY HIM OR HURL INSULTS UPON HIM, HE DID SO.

HIS SUPERIOR INTELLIGENCE AND CUNNING PERMITTED HIM TO INVENT A THOUSAND DIABOLICAL TRICKS TO ADD TO THE BURDENS OF TUBLAT'S LIFE. EARLY IN HIS BOYHOOD, HE HAD LEARNED TO FORM ROPES BY TWISTING AND TYING LONG GRASSES TOGETHER, AND WITH THESE HE WAS FOREVER TRIPPING TUBLAT OR ATTEMPTING TO HANG HIM FROM SOME OVERHANGING BRANCH.

BY PAINSTAKING PRACTISE HE LEARNED THE ART OF ROPING.

IT WAS A GERM OF THOUGHT FOR A MAGNIFICENT ACHIEVEMENT THAT WAS TO COME LATER.

AMUSING HIMSELF ONE DAY, THE NOOSE FELL SQUARELY ABOUT THE NECK OF A PLAYING COMPANION, BRINGING THE APE TO A SUDDEN AND SURPRISING HALT. AH, HERE WAS A FINE, NEW GAME, TARZAN THOUGHT. IF HE COULD CATCH HIS FELLOW APES WITH HIS LONG ARM OF MANY GRASSES, WHY NOT SABOR, THE LIONESS?

NOW, HOWEVER, THE LIFE OF TUBLAT WAS A LIVING NIGHTMARE. NIGHT OR DAY, HE NEVER KNEW WHEN THAT QUIET NOOSE WOULD SLIP ABOUT HIS NECK AND NEARLY CHOKE THE LIFE OUT OF HIM. TUBLAT SWORE DIRE VENGEANCE; KALA SCOLDED; AND TARZAN LAUGHED.

THE WANDERINGS OF THE TRIBE BROUGHT THEM OFTEN NEAR THE CLOSED AND SILENT CABIN. TO TARZAN THIS WAS A NEVER-ENDING SOURCE OF MYSTERY AND PLEASURE.

USUALLY HE WAS ALONE WHEN HE VISITED IT, FOR THE APES HAD NO LOVE FOR THE DESERTED ABODE. HE WOULD PEEK INTO THE WINDOWS OR CLIMB TO THE ROOF TO PEER DOWN THE CHIMNEY. BUT HE COULD FIND NO MEANS OF INGRESS.

THE STORY OF HIS OWN CONNECTION WITH THE CABIN HAD NEVER BEEN TOLD HIM. THE LANGUAGE OF THE APES HAS SO FEW WORDS THAT THEY COULD TALK BUT LITTLE OF WHAT THEY HAD SEEN IN THE CABIN. ONLY IN A DIM, VAGUE WAY HAD KALA EXPLAINED TO HIM THAT HIS FATHER HAD BEEN A STRANGE WHITE APE, BUT HE DID NOT KNOW THAT KALA WAS NOT HIS OWN MOTHER.

BUT ONE DAY TARZAN NOTICED THAT THE DOOR WAS AN INDEPENDENT PART OF THE WALL IN WHICH IT WAS SET, AND FOR THE FIRST TIME IT OCCURRED TO HIM THAT THIS MIGHT PROVE THE MEANS OF ENTRANCE WHICH HAD SO LONG ELUDED HIM.

ON THIS DAY, THEN, HE WENT DIRECTLY TO THE DOOR AND SPENT HOURS EXAMINING IT AND FUSSING WITH THE HINGES, THE KNOB, AND THE LATCH. FINALLY HE STUMBLED UPON THE RIGHT COMBINATION, AND THE DOOR SWUNG CREAKINGLY OPEN BEFORE HIS ASTONISHED EYES.

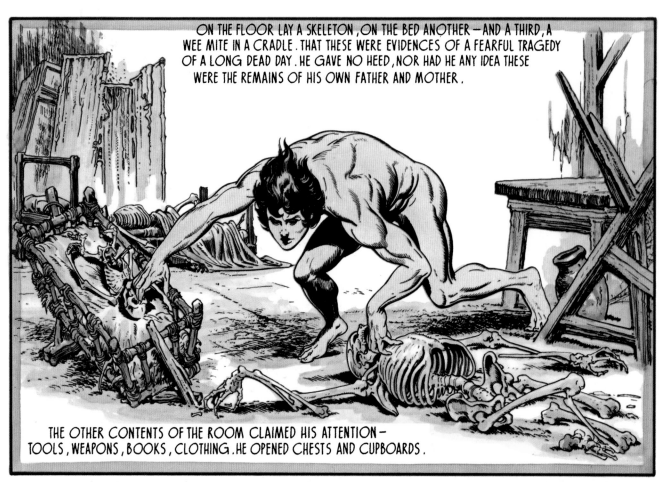

ON THE FLOOR LAY A SKELETON, ON THE BED ANOTHER — AND A THIRD, A WEE MITE IN A CRADLE. THAT THESE WERE EVIDENCES OF A FEARFUL TRAGEDY OF A LONG DEAD DAY. HE GAVE NO HEED, NOR HAD HE ANY IDEA THESE WERE THE REMAINS OF HIS OWN FATHER AND MOTHER.

THE OTHER CONTENTS OF THE ROOM CLAIMED HIS ATTENTION — TOOLS, WEAPONS, BOOKS, CLOTHING. HE OPENED CHESTS AND CUPBOARDS.

HE CAME UPON A SHARP HUNTING KNIFE, AND PROMPTLY CUT HIS FINGER.

UNDAUNTED, HE AMUSED HIMSELF WITH HIS NEW TOY, HACKING SPLINTERS FROM THE TABLE AND CHAIRS.

IN A CUPBOARD FILLED WITH BOOKS HE CAME ACROSS ONE WITH BRIGHTLY COLORED PICTURES — IT WAS A CHILD'S ILLUSTRATED ALPHABET —
A IS FOR ARCHER
B IS FOR BOY

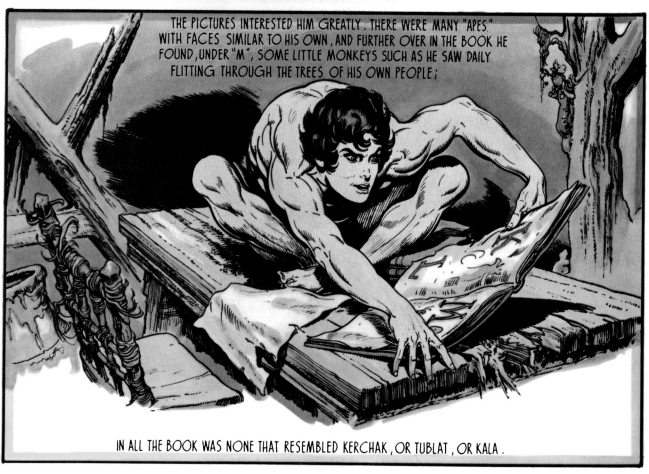

THE PICTURES INTERESTED HIM GREATLY. THERE WERE MANY "APES." WITH FACES SIMILAR TO HIS OWN, AND FURTHER OVER IN THE BOOK HE FOUND, UNDER "M", SOME LITTLE MONKEYS SUCH AS HE SAW DAILY FLITTING THROUGH THE TREES OF HIS OWN PEOPLE;

IN ALL THE BOOK WAS NONE THAT RESEMBLED KERCHAK, OR TUBLAT, OR KALA.

AT FIRST HE TRIED TO PICK THE LITTLE FIGURES FROM THE LEAVES, BUT HE SOON SAW THAT THEY WERE NOT REAL, THOUGH HE KNEW NOT WHAT THEY MIGHT BE, NOR HAD HE ANY WORDS TO DESCRIBE THEM. THE BOATS, AND TRAINS, AND COWS, AND HORSES WERE QUITE MEANINGLESS TO HIM, BUT NOT QUITE SO BAFFLING AS THE ODD LITTLE FIGURES WHICH APPEARED BENEATH AND BETWEEN THE COLORED PICTURES — SOME STRANGE KIND OF BUG HE THOUGHT THEY MIGHT BE, FOR MANY OF THEM HAD LEGS, THOUGH NOWHERE COULD HE FIND ONE WITH EYES AND A MOUTH.

IT WAS HIS FIRST INTRODUCTION TO THE LETTERS OF THE ALPHABET, AND HE WAS OVER TEN YEARS OLD. OF COURSE HE HAD NEVER BEFORE SEEN PRINT, NEVER HAD SPOKEN WITH ANY LIVING THING WHICH HAD THE REMOTEST IDEA THAT SUCH A THING AS A WRITTEN LANGUAGE EXISTED, NOR EVER HAD HE SEEN ANYONE READING. SO WHAT WONDER THAT THE LITTLE BOY WAS QUITE AT A LOSS TO GUESS THE MEANING OF THESE STRANGE FIGURES. NEAR THE MIDDLE OF THE BOOK HE FOUND HIS OLD ENEMY, SABOR, THE LIONESS, AND FURTHER ON, COILED HISTAH, THE SNAKE.

OH, IT WAS MOST ENGROSSING! NEVER BEFORE IN ALL HIS TEN YEARS HAD HE ENJOYED ANYTHING SO MUCH. SO ABSORBED WAS HE THAT HE DID NOT NOTE THE APPROACHING DUSK, UNTIL IT WAS QUITE UPON HIM AND THE FIGURES WERE BLURRED.

HE PUT THE BOOK BACK IN THE CUPBOARD AND CLOSED THE DOOR, FOR HE DID NOT WISH ANYONE ELSE TO FIND AND DESTROY HIS TREASURE, AND AS HE WENT OUT INTO THE GATHERING DARKNESS HE CLOSED THE GREAT DOOR OF THE CABIN BEHIND HIM AS IT HAD BEEN BEFORE HE DISCOVERED THE SECRET OF ITS LOCK. BUT BEFORE HE LEFT, HE HAD NOTICED THE HUNTING KNIFE LYING WHERE HE HAD THROWN IT UPON THE FLOOR, AND THIS HE PICKED UP AND TOOK WITH HIM TO SHOW TO HIS FELLOWS.

HE HAD TAKEN SCARCE A DOZEN STEPS TOWARD THE JUNGLE WHEN A GREAT FORM ROSE UP BEFORE HIM FROM THE SHADOWS OF A LOW BUSH. AT FIRST HE THOUGHT IT WAS ONE OF HIS OWN PEOPLE, BUT IN ANOTHER INSTANT HE REALIZED THAT IT WAS BOLGANI, THE HUGE GORILLA.

SO CLOSE WAS HE THAT THERE WAS NO CHANCE FOR FLIGHT AND LITTLE TARZAN KNEW THAT HE MUST STAND AND FIGHT FOR HIS LIFE, FOR THESE GREAT BEASTS WERE THE DEADLY ENEMIES OF HIS TRIBE, AND NEITHER ONE NOR THE OTHER EVER ASKED OR GAVE QUARTER.

HE WAS A BOY, BUT HE MET THE GORILLA WITHOUT A TRACE OF TREMOR OR PANIC. HE STRUCK THE CHARGING BRUTE WITH CLOSED FISTS. BUT IN ONE HAND HE CLUTCHED THE KNIFE. AS THE BRUTE LUNGED, ACCIDENTALLY THE KNIFE SANK DEEP INTO THE HAIRY BREAST.

BUT THE BOY HAD LEARNED IN THAT BRIEF SECOND A USE FOR HIS SHARP AND SHINING TOY, SO THAT, AS THE TEARING, STRIKING BEAST DRAGGED HIM TO THE EARTH, HE PLUNGED THE BLADE REPEATEDLY AND TO THE HILT INTO ITS BREAST.

THE GORILLA, FIGHTING AFTER THE MANNER OF ITS KIND, STRUCK TERRIFIC BLOWS WITH ITS OPEN HAND AND TORE THE FLESH AT THE BOY'S THROAT AND CHEST WITH ITS MIGHTY TUSKS.

FOR A MOMENT THEY ROLLED UPON THE GROUND IN THE FIERCE FRENZY OF COMBAT. MORE AND MORE WEAKLY THE TORN AND BLEEDING ARM STRUCK HOME WITH THE LONG SHARP BLADE, THEN THE LITTLE FIGURE STIFFENED WITH A SPASMODIC JERK, AND TARZAN, THE YOUNG LORD GREYSTOKE, ROLLED BACK UPON THE DEAD AND DECAYING VEGETATION WHICH CARPETED HIS JUNGLE HOME.

BACK IN THE FOREST THE TRIBE HAD HEARD THE FIERCE CHALLENGE OF THE GORILLA. AND
KALA, SEEING THAT TARZAN WAS MISSING, FAIRLY FLEW THROUGH THE TREES. DARKNESS
HAD NOW FALLEN, AND AN EARLY MOON WAS SENDING ITS FAINT LIGHT TO CAST
STRANGE, GROTESQUE SHADOWS AMONG THE DENSE FOLIAGE OF THE FOREST.

LIKE SOME HUGE PHANTOM,
KALA SWUNG NOISELESSLY FROM
TREE TO TREE; NOW RUNNING NIMBLY
ALONG A GREAT BRANCH, NOW
SWINGING THROUGH SPACE AT THE END
OF ANOTHER, IN HER RAPID PROGRESS. THAT
HER LITTLE TARZAN COULD DESTROY A GREAT
BULL GORILLA SHE KNEW TO BE IMPROBABLE, AND
SO, AS SHE NEARED THE SPOT FROM WHICH THE
SOUNDS OF THE STRUGGLE HAD COME, SHE MOVED
WITH EXTREME CAUTION AS SHE TRAVERSED THE LOWEST
BRANCHES, PEERING EAGERLY INTO THE MOON-SPLASHED
BLACKNESS FOR A SIGN OF THE COMBATANTS.

PRESENTLY SHE CAME UPON THEM, LYING IN A LITTLE OPEN SPACE FULL UNDER THE BRILLIANT LIGHT OF THE MOON — LITTLE TARZAN'S TORN AND BLOODY FORM, AND BESIDE IT A GREAT BULL GORILLA, STONE DEAD.

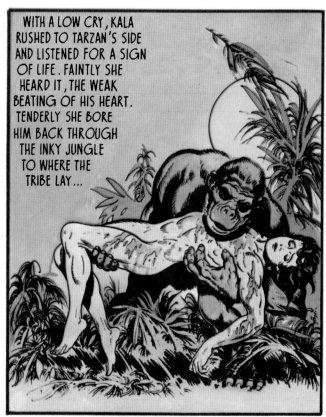

WITH A LOW CRY, KALA RUSHED TO TARZAN'S SIDE AND LISTENED FOR A SIGN OF LIFE. FAINTLY SHE HEARD IT, THE WEAK BEATING OF HIS HEART. TENDERLY SHE BORE HIM BACK THROUGH THE INKY JUNGLE TO WHERE THE TRIBE LAY...

...AND FOR MANY DAYS AND NIGHTS SHE SAT GUARD BESIDE HIM, BRINGING HIM FOOD AND WATER, AND BRUSHING THE FLIES AND OTHER INSECTS FROM HIS CRUEL WOUNDS.

OF MEDICINE OR SURGERY THE
POOR THING KNEW NOTHING. SHE
COULD BUT LICK THE WOUNDS, AND THUS
SHE KEPT THEM CLEANSED, THAT HEALING
NATURE MIGHT THE MORE QUICKLY DO
HER WORK. AT FIRST TARZAN WOULD EAT
NOTHING, BUT ROLLED AND TOSSED IN A
WILD DELIRIUM OF FEVER. ALL HE CRAVED
WAS WATER, AND THIS SHE BROUGHT HIM IN
THE ONLY WAY SHE COULD, BEARING IT IN HER OWN MOUTH.

NO HUMAN MOTHER COULD HAVE SHOWN MORE UNSELFISH
AND SACRIFICING DEVOTION THAN DID THIS POOR, WILD BRUTE
FOR THE LITTLE ORPHANED WAIF WHOM FATE HAD THROWN INTO HER KEEPING.

AT LAST THE FEVER ABATED AND THE BOY COMMENCED TO MEND. NO WORD OF
COMPLAINT PASSED HIS TIGHT SET LIPS, THOUGH THE PAIN OF HIS WOUNDS WAS
EXCRUCIATING. WITH THE STOICISM OF THE BRUTES WHO HAD RAISED HIM, HE
ENDURED HIS SUFFERING QUIETLY, PREFERRING TO CRAWL AWAY FROM THE OTHERS
AND LIE HUDDLED IN SOME CLUMP OF TALL GRASSES RATHER THAN TO SHOW HIS
MISERY BEFORE THEIR EYES. KALA, ALONE, HE WAS GLAD TO HAVE WITH HIM, BUT
NOW THAT HE WAS BETTER SHE WAS GONE LONGER AT A TIME, IN SEARCH OF
FOOD; FOR THE DEVOTED ANIMAL HAD SCARCELY EATEN ENOUGH TO SUPPORT
HER OWN LIFE WHILE TARZAN HAD BEEN SO LOW, AND SHE WAS, IN CONSEQUENCE,
REDUCED TO A MERE SHADOW OF HER FORMER SELF.

AFTER WHAT SEEMED AN ETERNITY TO THE LITTLE
SUFFERER, HE WAS ABLE TO WALK ONCE MORE, AND
FROM THEN ON HIS RECOVERY WAS RAPID, SO THAT
IN ANOTHER MONTH HE WAS AS STRONG AND ACTIVE
AS EVER. DURING HIS CONVALESCENCE, HE HAD GONE
OVER IN HIS MIND MANY TIMES THE BATTLE WITH THE
GORILLA, AND HIS FIRST THOUGHT WAS TO RECOVER
THE WONDERFUL LITTLE WEAPON WHICH HAD TRANSFORMED
HIM FROM A HOPELESSLY OUTCLASSED WEAKLING
TO THE SUPERIOR OF THE MIGHTY TERROR OF
THE JUNGLE.

THUS DID TARZAN END THE FIRST, CURIOUS
CHAPTER OF HIS YOUNG LIFE. AN EVEN STRANGER
ONE WAS TO FOLLOW.

BOOK TWO

OF THE APES

AFTER A SEARCH NEAR THE BONES OF HIS GREAT ADVERSARY HE FOUND THE FORMIDABLE KNIFE NOW RED WITH RUST.

NOW, FULLY RECOVERED FROM HIS BATTLE WITH BOLGANI THE GORILLA, TARZAN BECAME ANXIOUS TO RETURN TO THE CABIN WITH ITS WONDROUS CONTENTS. ONE MORNING HE SET FORTH ON HIS QUEST.

IN ANOTHER MOMENT HE WAS AT THE CABIN, AND HAD THROWN THE LATCH AND ENTERED. HIS FIRST CONCERN WAS TO LEARN THE MECHANISM OF THE LOCK SO THAT HE COULD LEARN PRECISELY WHAT CAUSED IT TO HOLD THE DOOR. HE FOUND THAT HE COULD CLOSE AND LOCK THE DOOR FROM WITHIN, AND THIS HE DID SO THAT THERE WOULD BE NO CHANCE OF HIS BEING MOLESTED WHILE AT HIS INVESTIGATIONS.

HE COMMENCED A SYSTEMATIC SEARCH OF THE CABIN; BUT HIS ATTENTION WAS SOON RIVETED BY THE BOOKS ...

... WHICH SEEMED TO EXERT A STRANGE AND POWERFUL INFLUENCE OVER HIM.

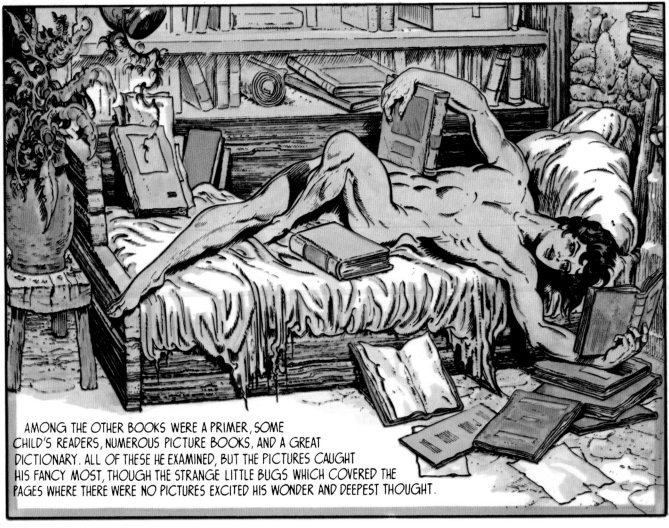

AMONG THE OTHER BOOKS WERE A PRIMER, SOME CHILD'S READERS, NUMEROUS PICTURE BOOKS, AND A GREAT DICTIONARY. ALL OF THESE HE EXAMINED, BUT THE PICTURES CAUGHT HIS FANCY MOST, THOUGH THE STRANGE LITTLE BUGS WHICH COVERED THE PAGES WHERE THERE WERE NO PICTURES EXCITED HIS WONDER AND DEEPEST THOUGHT.

SQUATTING UPON HIS HAUNCHES ON THE TABLE TOP IN THE CABIN HIS FATHER HAD BUILT -- HIS SMOOTH, BROWN, NAKED LITTLE BODY BENT OVER THE BOOK WHICH RESTED IN HIS STRONG SLENDER HANDS, AND HIS GREAT SHOCK OF LONG, BLACK HAIR FALLING ABOUT HIS WELL-SHAPED HEAD AND BRIGHT, INTELLIGENT EYES -- TARZAN OF THE APES, LITTLE PRIMITIVE MAN, PRESENTED A PICTURE FILLED, AT ONCE, WITH PATHOS AND WITH PROMISE -- AN ALLEGORICAL FIGURE OF THE PRIMORDIAL GROPING THROUGH THE BLACK NIGHT OF IGNORANCE TOWARD THE LIGHT OF LEARNING. HIS LITTLE FACE WAS TENSE IN STUDY, FOR HE HAD PARTIALLY GRASPED, IN A HAZY, NEBULOUS WAY, THE RUDIMENTS OF A THOUGHT WHICH WAS DESTINED TO PROVE THE KEY AND THE SOLUTION TO THE PUZZLING PROBLEM OF THE STRANGE LITTLE BUGS.

HOGARTH=

IN HIS HANDS WAS A PRIMER OPENED AT A PICTURE OF A LITTLE APE SIMILAR TO HIMSELF, BUT COVERED, EXCEPT FOR HANDS AND FACE, WITH STRANGE, COLORED FUR, FOR SUCH HE THOUGHT THE JACKET AND TROUSERS TO BE. BENEATH THE PICTURE WERE THREE LITTLE BUGS -- B O Y.

AND NOW HE HAD DISCOVERED IN THE TEXT UPON THE PAGE THAT THESE THREE WERE REPEATED MANY TIMES IN THE SAME SEQUENCE. ANOTHER FACT HE LEARNED -- THAT THERE WERE COMPARATIVELY FEW INDIVIDUAL BUGS; BUT THESE WERE REPEATED MANY TIMES, OCCASIONALLY ALONE, BUT MORE OFTEN IN COMPANY WITH OTHERS.

SLOWLY HE TURNED THE PAGES, SCANNING THE PICTURES AND THE TEXT FOR A REPETITION OF THE COMBINATION B-O-Y. PRESENTLY HE FOUND IT BENEATH A PICTURE OF ANOTHER LITTLE APE AND A STRANGE ANIMAL WHICH WENT UPON FOUR LEGS LIKE THE JACKAL AND RESEMBLED HIM NOT A LITTLE. BENEATH THIS PICTURE THE BUGS APPEARED AS: A BOY AND A DOG. THERE THEY WERE, THE THREE LITTLE BUGS WHICH ALWAYS ACCOMPANIED THE LITTLE APE.

AND SO HE PROGRESSED VERY, VERY SLOWLY, FOR IT WAS A HARD AND LABORIOUS TASK WHICH HE HAD SET HIMSELF WITHOUT KNOWING IT -- A TASK WHICH MIGHT SEEM TO YOU OR ME IMPOSSIBLE -- LEARNING TO READ WITHOUT HAVING THE SLIGHTEST KNOWLEDGE OF LETTERS OR WRITTEN LANGUAGE, OR THE FAINTEST IDEA THAT SUCH THINGS EXISTED.

HE DID NOT ACCOMPLISH IT IN A DAY, OR IN A WEEK, OR IN A MONTH, OR IN A YEAR, BUT SLOWLY, VERY SLOWLY, HE LEARNED AFTER HE HAD GRASPED THE POSSIBILITIES WHICH LAY IN THOSE LITTLE BUGS...

... SO THAT BY THE TIME HE WAS FIFTEEN HE KNEW THE VARIOUS COMBINATIONS OF LETTERS WHICH STOOD FOR EVERY PRINTED FIGURE IN THE LITTLE PRIMER AND IN ONE OR TWO OF THE PICTURE BOOKS.

HOGARTH.

ONE DAY WHEN HE WAS ABOUT TWELVE, HE FOUND A NUMBER OF LEAD PENCILS, AND HE WAS DELIGHTED TO DISCOVER THE BLACK LINE ONE OF THEM LEFT WHEN IT WAS SCRATCHED ON THE TABLE TOP.

SOON, AFTER A MASS OF SCRAWLY LOOPS, HE ATTEMPTED TO REPRODUCE THE BUGS HE SAW IN HIS BOOKS. IT WAS A DIFFICULT TASK, BUT HE HAD MADE A BEGINNING AT WRITING.

HE PERSEVERED FOR MONTHS. AND BY THE TIME HE WAS SEVENTEEN, HE HAD LEARNED THE WONDERFUL PURPOSE OF THE BOOKS WITH THE BUGS

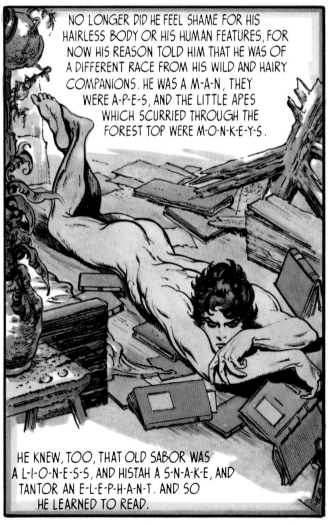

NO LONGER DID HE FEEL SHAME FOR HIS HAIRLESS BODY OR HIS HUMAN FEATURES, FOR NOW HIS REASON TOLD HIM THAT HE WAS OF A DIFFERENT RACE FROM HIS WILD AND HAIRY COMPANIONS. HE WAS A M-A-N, THEY WERE A-P-E-S, AND THE LITTLE APES WHICH SCURRIED THROUGH THE FOREST TOP WERE M-O-N-K-E-Y-S.

HE KNEW, TOO, THAT OLD SABOR WAS A L-I-O-N-E-S-S, AND HISTAH A S-N-A-K-E, AND TANTOR AN E-L-E-P-H-A-N-T. AND SO HE LEARNED TO READ.

THERE WERE MANY BREAKS IN HIS EDUCATION, CAUSED BY THE MIGRATORY HABITS OF HIS TRIBE, BUT EVEN WHEN REMOVED FROM RECOURSE TO HIS BOOKS, HIS ACTIVE BRAIN CONTINUED TO SEARCH OUT THE MYSTERIES OF THE FASCINATING BUGS.

PIECES OF BARK AND FLAT LEAVES AND EVEN SMOOTH STRETCHES OF BARE EARTH PROVIDED HIM WITH COPY BOOKS WHEREON TO SCRATCH WITH THE POINT OF HIS HUNTING KNIFE THE LESSONS HE WAS LEARNING. NOR DID HE NEGLECT THE STERNER DUTIES OF LIFE WHILE FOLLOWING THE BENT OF HIS INCLINATION TOWARD THE SOLVING OF THE MYSTERY OF HIS LIBRARY.

HE PRACTICED WITH HIS ROPE AND PLAYED WITH HIS SHARP KNIFE, WHICH HE HAD LEARNED TO KEEP KEEN BY WHETTING UPON FLAT STONES.

THE TRIBE HAD GROWN LARGER SINCE TARZAN HAD COME AMONG THEM, FOR UNDER THE LEADERSHIP OF KERCHAK THEY HAD PLENTY TO EAT AND LITTLE OR NO LOSS FROM PREDATORY INCURSIONS OF NEIGHBORS. THE YOUNGER MALES AS THEY BECAME ADULT FOUND IT MORE COMFORTABLE TO LIVE IN AMITY WITH KERCHAK RATHER THAN ATTEMPT TO SET UP A NEW ESTABLISHMENT OF THEIR OWN OR FIGHT WITH THE REDOUBTABLE BULL FOR SUPREMACY AT HOME. OCCASIONALLY ONE MORE FEROCIOUS THAN HIS FELLOWS WOULD ATTEMPT THIS LATTER ALTERNATIVE, BUT NONE HAD COME YET WHO COULD WREST THE PALM OF VICTORY FROM THE FIERCE AND BRUTAL APE.

TARZAN NOW HELD A PECULIAR POSITION IN THE TRIBE, BUT ONE DAY TARZAN AT LAST ESTABLISHED HIS RIGHT TO RESPECT. THE TRIBE WAS GATHERED ABOUT A SMALL NATURAL AMPHITHEATER IN WHOSE CENTER WAS A STRANGE EARTHEN DRUM.

HERE THE TRIBE PERFORMED THE RITUAL OF THE DUM-DUM -- AND TODAY IT MARKED THE KILLING OF A GIANT APE, A MEMBER OF ANOTHER TRIBE. MANY TRAVELERS HAVE SEEN THE DRUMS OF THE GREAT APES, AND SOME HAVE HEARD THE SOUNDS OF THEIR BEATING AND THE NOISE OF THE WILD, WEIRD REVELRY OF THESE FIRST LORDS OF THE JUNGLE, BUT TARZAN, LORD GREYSTOKE, IS, DOUBTLESS, THE ONLY HUMAN BEING WHO EVER JOINED IN THE FIERCE, MAD, INTOXICATING REVEL OF THE DUM-DUM.

CEREMONIOUSLY, THE PEOPLE OF KERCHAK LAID THEIR BURDEN BEFORE THE EARTHEN DRUM, AND SQUATTED BESIDE IT AS GUARDS. FOR A TIME ABSOLUTE QUIET REIGNED IN THE CLEARING --

--UNTIL THE RISING MOON GAVE THE SIGNAL FOR THE SAVAGE ORGY. NOW THREE OLD FEMALES BEGAN TAPPING ON THE RESOUNDING SURFACE OF THE DRUM, EACH WITH A KNOTTED BRANCH.

THE GREAT CIRCLE OF APES MOVED TO THE RHYTHMIC DIN AND FREQUENCY OF THEIR BLOWS, UNTIL THE JUNGLE ECHOED IN EVERY DIRECTION.

HUGE, FIERCE BRUTES STOPPED IN THEIR HUNTING, WITH UPPRICKED EARS AND RAISED HEADS, TO LISTEN TO THE DULL BOOMING THAT BETOKENED THE DUM-DUM OF THE APES.

AS THE SAVAGE DIN ROSE TO AN ALMOST DEAFENING VOLUME KERCHAK SPRANG INTO THE OPEN SPACE. HE THREW BACK HIS HEAD, BEAT UPON HIS CHEST AND EMITTED THREE FEARFUL SHRIEKS.

NOW ONE AFTER ANOTHER IN QUICK SUCCESSION THE APES REPEATED THE HORRID CRIES OF THE KING.

THE GREAT CIRCLE
MOVED IN THE MAD WHIRL
OF THE DUM-DUM DANCE OF
DEATH. TARZAN, SWEAT-STREAKED
AND GLISTENING IN THE MOONLIGHT,
BECAME ONE WITH THE WILD,
LEAPING HORDE.

AT A SIGN FROM KERCHAK, THE DRUMS CEASED. THEN AS ONE, THE MALES RUSHED HEADLONG UPON THE DEAD APE AND WITH BLOWS REDUCED IT TO A HAIRY PULP. GREAT FANGS SANK INTO THE CARCASS, THE MIGHTIEST OF THE APES SEIZING THE CHOICEST MORSELS.

TARZAN WORMED INTO THE STRUGGLING MASS OF APES, AND WITH HIS KNIFE SLASHED OFF A PORTION MORE THAN HE HAD HOPED FOR.

BUT OLD TUBLAT, KALA'S MATE AND TARZAN'S ENEMY, SPIED THE BOY CLUTCHING HIS PRIZE. WITH A WICKED GLEAM OF HATE HE MADE FOR HIM.

BUT TARZAN LEAPED NIMBLY AWAY, WITH HIS ARCH ENEMY CLOSE UPON HIS HEELS.

SWIFTLY HE SPED TOWARD THE SURROUNDING TREES, SPRANG TO A LOWER LIMB --

--AND CLIMBED RAPIDLY UPWARD TO THE WAVING PINNACLE OF A LOFTY GIANT. THE HEAVY TUBLAT DARED NOT FOLLOW. THERE TARZAN PERCHED, HURLING INSULTS AT THE RAGING BRUTE BELOW.

AND THEN TUBLAT WENT MAD. WITH HORRIFYING SCREAMS AND ROARS HE RUSHED TO THE GROUND AMONG THE FEMALES AND YOUNG, SINKING HIS FANGS INTO A DOZEN NECKS.

FROM ABOVE TARZAN WITNESSED THE MAD CARNIVAL OF RAGE. THEN TUBLAT SPIED A FEMALE MAKING FOR THE TREE WHERE TARZAN PERCHED. IT WAS KALA.

CLOSE BEHIND HER CAME THE AWFUL TUBLAT. AND AS QUICKLY TARZAN DROPPED LIKE A STONE TOWARD HIS FOSTER MOTHER.

WITH A ROAR TUBLAT LEAPED AS KALA SPRANG FOR AN OVERHANGING LIMB ALMOST ABOVE HIS HEAD. AND SHE WOULD HAVE BEEN SAFE --

-- BUT THERE WAS A SUDDEN, TEARING SOUND. THE BRANCH BROKE, AND DOWN SHE CAME ON THE HEAD OF TUBLAT, KNOCKING HIM TO THE GROUND.

IN THAT INSTANT THE MAN-CHILD PLUNGED BETWEEN HIS FOSTER MOTHER AND THE INFURIATED BULL. NOTHING COULD HAVE SUITED THE FIERCE BEAST BETTER.

THE MORNING AFTER THE DUM-DUM THE TRIBE STARTED SLOWLY BACK THROUGH THE FOREST.

THE MARCH WAS A LEISURELY SEARCH FOR FOOD. ONCE OLD SABOR CROSSED THEIR PATH, AND THEY MOVED TO THE SAFETY OF THE HIGHER BRANCHES.

UPON A LOW-HANGING BRANCH SAT TARZAN. HE HURLED A PINEAPPLE, TAUNTING THE ANCIENT ENEMY OF HIS PEOPLE. WITH A LASH OF HER TAIL SHE BARED HER FANGS IN A HIDEOUS SNARL.

FOR A MOMENT THE TWO EYED EACH OTHER IN FIERCE CHALLENGE. IN TARZAN'S MIND A GREAT PLAN HAD SPRUNG. HE HAD KILLED MIGHTY TUBLAT; NOW HE WOULD TRACK DOWN THE CRAFTY SABOR AND SLAY HER LIKEWISE.

ABOVE EVERYTHING HE DESIRED SABOR'S SKIN TO COVER HIS NAKEDNESS WITH *CLOTHES*. HE HAD LEARNED FROM HIS PICTURE BOOKS THAT ALL *MEN* WERE SO COVERED.

DAYS AFTER HE HAD THOUGHT OF LITTLE ELSE.

ON THIS DAY, MORE IMMEDIATE INTERESTS WERE TO ATTRACT HIS ATTENTION. OF A SUDDEN IT BECAME AS MIDNIGHT; THE NOISES OF THE JUNGLE CEASED; THE TREES STOOD MOTIONLESS AS THOUGH IN PARALYZED EXPECTANCY OF SOME IMMINENT DANGER. ALL NATURE WAITED...

...BUT NOT FOR LONG. SUDDENLY, WITH AN AWESOME MOANING OF THE WIND, A VIVID AND BLINDING LIGHT AND A CANNONADE OF ROARING THUNDER, A STORM BROKE. THE TREES BENT, THEIR MIGHTY TOPS LASHING, AS THE DELUGE FELL UPON THE JUNGLE. FOR HOURS IT RAGED, WHILE THE TRIBE HUDDLED IN MISERY, SHIVERING FROM RAIN, COLD AND FEAR.

THE END WAS AS SUDDEN AS THE BEGINNING. THE WIND
CEASED, THE SUN SHONE FORTH--NATURE SMILED ONCE MORE.
THE DRIPPING LEAVES AND THE MOIST PETALS OF FLOWERS GLISTENED
IN THE SPLENDOR OF THE RETURNING DAY. NATURE FORGOT, HER CHILDREN
FORGOT, ALSO. BUSY LIFE WENT ON AS IT HAD BEEN BEFORE THE DARKNESS AND FRIGHT

BUT TO TARZAN A DAWNING LIGHT HAD COME TO EXPLAIN THE MYSTERY ABOUT
CLOTHES. HOW SNUG HE WOULD HAVE BEEN UNDER THE HEAVY COAT OF
SABOR! AND SO WAS ADDED A FURTHER INCENTIVE TO THE ADVENTURE.

ALWAYS WHEN JOURNEYING, TARZAN HAD KEPT HIS ROPE IN READINESS, PRACTISING WITH THE QUICK THROWN NOOSE.

ONCE HE SNARED HORTA, THE BOAR...

...AND ITS MAD LUNGE TOPPLED TARZAN FROM HIS PERCH. HE LOST A ROPE ON THIS OCCASION, BUT HAD IT BEEN SABOR WHO DRAGGED HIM DOWN, DOUBTLESS HE WOULD HAVE LOST HIS LIFE.

THUS BY EXPERIENCE HE LEARNED THE LIMITATIONS AS WELL AS THE POSSIBILITIES OF HIS STRANGE NEW WEAPON. IT TOOK HIM MANY DAYS TO BRAID A NEW ROPE, BUT WHEN IT WAS DONE, HE WENT FORTH PURPOSELY TO HUNT...

...TO LIE IN WAIT IN THE FOLIAGE OF A GREAT BRANCH ABOVE THE TRAIL THAT LED TO WATER.

SEVERAL SMALL ANIMALS PASSED UNHARMED BENEATH HIM. HE DID NOT WANT SUCH INSIGNIFICANT GAME. IT WOULD TAKE A STRONG ANIMAL TO TEST THE EFFICACY OF HIS NEW SCHEME.

AT LAST CAME SHE WHOM TARZAN SOUGHT, WITH SINEWS ROLLING BENEATH SHIMMERING HIDE; FAT AND GLOSSY CAME SABOR, THE LIONESS.

HER GREAT PADDED FEET FELL SOFT AND NOISELESS ON THE NARROW TRAIL. HER HEAD WAS HIGH IN EVER ALERT ATTENTION; HER LONG TAIL MOVED SLOWLY IN SINUOUS AND GRACEFUL UNDULATIONS. NEARER AND NEARER SHE CAME TO WHERE TARZAN OF THE APES CROUCHED UPON HIS LIMB, THE COILS OF HIS LONG ROPE POISED READY IN HIS HAND.

LIKE A THING OF BRONZE, MOTIONLESS AS DEATH, SAT TARZAN AS SABOR PASSED BENEATH.

THEN THE SILENT COIL SHOT OUT LIKE A GREAT SNAKE, LOOPED THE GLOSSY THROAT, AND WITH A JERK TARZAN DREW THE NOOSE TIGHT. SABOR WAS TRAPPED.

WITH A BOUND THE STARTLED BEAST TURNED INTO THE JUNGLE, BUT TARZAN WAS NOT TO LOSE ANOTHER ROPE THROUGH THE SAME CAUSE AS THE FIRST. THE LIONESS HAD TAKEN BUT HALF HER SECOND BOUND WHEN SHE FELT THE ROPE TIGHTEN; HER BODY TURNED COMPLETELY OVER IN THE AIR AND SHE FELL WITH A CRASH UPON HER BACK. TARZAN HAD FASTENED THE END OF THE ROPE TO THE TRUNK OF THE GREAT TREE ON WHICH HE SAT.

BUT SABOR NOW FOUND IT WAS ONLY A SLENDER CORD THAT HELD HER, AND GRASPING IT IN HER JAWS SHE SEVERED IT, AND WAS FREE.

TARZAN MOCKED AND TAUNTED THE PACING, ROARING CREATURE, BUT HE WAS MUCH CHAGRINED. THE WELL-LAID PLAN HAD COME TO NAUGHT.

HOGARTH=

AT LAST, WITH A PARTING CHALLENGE AND A WELL-AIMED RIPE FRUIT INTO THE FACE OF HIS ADVERSARY, HE SWUNG AWAY TOWARD THE MEMBERS OF HIS TRIBE. IT WAS NOT THE LAST ENCOUNTER WITH SABOR, HE KNEW. THEY WOULD MEET AGAIN.

TARZAN OF THE APES
LIVED ON IN HIS WILD, JUNGLE
EXISTENCE WITH LITTLE
CHANGE EXCEPT THAT HE
GREW STRONGER AND WISER,
AND FROM HIS BOOKS LEARNED
MORE OF THE STRANGE
WORLDS WHICH LAY
SOMEWHERE OUTSIDE
HIS PRIMEVAL FOREST.

WITH TANTOR THE ELEPHANT HE HAD MADE FRIENDS, AND ON MANY
MOONLIT NIGHTS THEY WALKED TOGETHER, OR WHERE IT WAS
CLEAR, HE RODE ON TANTOR'S MIGHTY BACK.

THUS, AT EIGHTEEN, WHILE HE COULD READ AND WRITE ENGLISH, TARZAN
SPOKE NO HUMAN LANGUAGE -- ONLY THAT OF THE BEASTS -- SINCE HE HAD
NEVER SEEN A HUMAN BEING OTHER THAN HIMSELF. SO IT HAPPENED ONE DAY THAT
THE SECURITY OF HIS JUNGLE WAS BROKEN FOREVER, WHEN THERE APPEARED A STRANGE
CAVALCADE, STRUNG IN SINGLE FILE, OVER THE BROW OF A LOW HILL.

IN ADVANCE WERE FIFTY WARRIORS ARMED WITH SPEARS, LONG BOWS, AND POISONED ARROWS. THEN CAME SEVERAL HUNDRED WOMEN AND CHILDREN BEARING BURDENS AND UTENSILS, AND BEHIND, A LARGE REAR GUARD. IT WAS CLEAR THAT THEY FEARED AN ATTACK. INDEED, THEY WERE FLEEING FROM A FORCE OF SOLDIERS SEEKING VENGEANCE FOR A MASSACRE OF TROOPS WHO HAD HARASSED THEM FOR IVORY.

INTO THE UNTRACKED JUNGLE THEY MARCHED, THIS REMNANT OF A ONCE POWERFUL TRIBE, TOWARD THE UNKNOWN AND FREEDOM. AT A CLEARING NEAR A RIVER THEY SET TO WORK TO BUILD A VILLAGE, ERECTING HUTS AND PALISADES. IN A MONTH THEY HAD TAKEN UP LIFE IN THEIR NEW HOME. HERE THERE WERE NO WHITE MEN, NO SOLDIERS, NO RUBBER OR IVORY TO BE GATHERED FOR CRUEL AND THANKLESS TASKMASTERS.

SEVERAL MOONS PASSED ERE THE BLACKS VENTURED BEYOND THE VILLAGE STOCKADE. BUT ONE DAY KULONGA, THE KING'S SON, WANDERED INTO THE DENSE MAZES OF THE FOREST, EQUIPPED WITH BOW AND POISONED ARROWS, HIS LANCE AND SHIELD READY.

NIGHT FOUND HIM FAR FROM THE VILLAGE; SO HE MADE A RUDE PLATFORM IN A TREE AND CURLED UP TO SLEEP.

THE NEXT DAWN, NEARBY, THE TRIBE OF KERCHAK WAS ASTIR SEARCHING FOR FOOD. TARZAN LEISURELY HUNTED. AND KALA ...

...BUSILY ENGAGED DOWNTRAIL, WAS STARTLED BY A FAINT, STRANGE NOISE. FULL FIFTY YARDS BEFORE HER, SHE SAW THE STEALTHY ADVANCE OF A STRANGE AND FEARSOME CREATURE. IT WAS KULONGA.

KALA TURNED AND MOVED RAPIDLY BACK ALONG THE TRAIL.

SHE SOUGHT TO AVOID RATHER THAN ESCAPE. CLOSE AFTER HER CAME KULONGA. HERE WAS MEAT AND HE WAS HUNGRY. ON HE HURRIED, HIS SPEAR POISED FOR THE THROW.

AT A BEND IN THE TRAIL, HIS ARM SHOT BACK. LIGHTNING-LIKE THE SPEAR SPED TOWARD KALA.

BUT IT GRAZED HER SIDE. WITH A CRY OF RAGE, SHE TURNED UPON HER TORMENTOR.

HOGARTH

AS SHE CHARGED, KULONGA UNSLUNG HIS BOW, FITTED AN ARROW AND DROVE THE POISONED MISSLE INTO THE HEART OF THE GREAT ANTHROPOID.

IN THE TREES THE APES SWUNG RAPIDLY TOWARD THE PLACE OF KALA'S HORRID SCREAM. BEFORE THE ASTONISHED MEMBERS OF THE TRIBE, KALA PLUNGED FORWARD ON HER FACE.

ROARING, THEY DASHED TOWARD KULONGA. BUT THE WARY HUNTER WAS DARTING AWAY LIKE A FRIGHTENED ANTELOPE.

TARZAN'S GRIEF AND ANGER WERE UNBOUNDED. HE ROARED OUT HIS HIDEOUS CHALLENGE TIME AND AGAIN. HE BEAT UPON HIS GREAT
CHEST WITH HIS CLENCHED FISTS, AND THEN HE FELL UPON THE BODY OF KALA AND SOBBED OUT THE PITIFUL SORROWING OF HIS
LONELY HEART. TO LOSE THE ONLY CREATURE IN ALL ONE'S WORLD WHO EVER HAD MANIFESTED LOVE AND AFFECTION FOR ONE IS
A GREAT BEREAVEMENT INDEED. WHAT THOUGH KALA WAS A FIERCE AND HIDEOUS APE! TO TARZAN SHE HAD BEEN KIND, SHE HAD BEEN
BEAUTIFUL. UPON HER HE HAD LAVISHED, UNKNOWN TO HIMSELF, ALL THE REVERENCE AND RESPECT AND LOVE THAT A NORMAL ENGLISH
BOY FEELS FOR HIS OWN MOTHER. HE HAD NEVER KNOWN ANOTHER, AND SO TO KALA WAS GIVEN, THOUGH
MUTELY, ALL THAT WOULD HAVE BELONGED TO THE FAIR AND LOVELY LADY ALICE HAD SHE LIVED.

AFTER THE OUTBURST OF GRIEF, TARZAN
QUESTIONED THE MEMBERS OF THE TRIBE
WHO HAD WITNESSED THE KILLING OF KALA.

HE LEARNED ALL THAT THEIR MEAGER VOCABULARY COULD VOUCHSAFE HIM. IT WAS ENOUGH, HOWEVER, FOR HIS NEEDS. IT TOLD
HIM OF A STRANGE, HAIRLESS, BLACK APE WITH FEATHERS GROWING UPON ITS HEAD, WHO LAUNCHED DEATH FROM A SLENDER
BRANCH, AND THEN RAN, WITH THE FLEETNESS OF BARA, THE DEER, TOWARD THE RISING SUN.

TARZAN WAITED NO LONGER, BUT LEAPING INTO THE BRANCHES
OF THE TREES SPED RAPIDLY THROUGH THE FOREST, TO INTERCEPT THE
BLACK WARRIOR WHO WAS EVIDENTLY FOLLOWING THE TORTUOUS DETOURS OF THE TRAIL.

IN AN HOUR HE CAME UPON THE TRAIL.
IN THE SOFT MUD ON THE BANK OF A TINY
RIVULET HE FOUND FOOTPRINTS SUCH AS HE
ALONE IN ALL THE JUNGLE HAD EVER MADE, BUT MUCH
LARGER THAN HIS. HIS HEART BEAT FAST. COULD IT BE
THAT HE WAS TRAILING A *MAN*--ONE OF HIS OWN RACE?

HE SPED OFF. BARELY A MILE BEYOND,
HE CAME UPON THE BLACK WARRIOR.
OPPOSITE HIM STOOD HORTA, THE BOAR,
READY TO CHARGE. TARZAN LOOKED WITH
WONDER UPON THE STRANGE *CREATURE* BENEATH HIM...

... SO LIKE HIM IN FORM
AND YET SO DIFFERENT IN FACE
AND COLOR. HIS BOOKS HAD PORTRAYED
THE *NEGRO*, BUT HOW DIFFERENT HAD BEEN THE
DULL, DEAD PRINT TO THIS SLEEK FIGURE OF EBONY, PULSING WITH LIFE.

HORTA CHARGED AS KULONGA DODGED, AND SENT AN ARROW INTO ITS BACK. THE BOAR STAGGERED--AND FELL.

TARZAN WATCHED AS KULONGA CUT SEVERAL STRIPS FROM THE BOAR'S BODY, BUILT A FIRE, AND ATE HIS FILL.

TARZAN'S DESIRE TO KILL BURNED FIERCELY IN HIS WILD BREAST, BUT HIS DESIRE TO LEARN WAS EVEN GREATER. HE WOULD FOLLOW THIS STRANGE CREATURE FOR A WHILE AND KNOW FROM WHENCE HE CAME. HE COULD KILL HIM AT HIS LEISURE LATER, WHEN THE BOW AND DEADLY ARROWS WERE LAID ASIDE.

WHEN KULONGA HAD FINISHED HIS REPAST AND
DISAPPEARED BEYOND A NEAR TURNING OF THE
PATH, TARZAN DROPPED QUICKLY TO THE GROUND.
WITH HIS KNIFE HE SEVERED MANY STRIPS OF MEAT FROM
HORTA'S CARCASS, BUT HE DID NOT COOK THEM.

HE HAD SEEN FIRE, BUT
ONLY WHEN ARA, THE
LIGHTNING, HAD
DESTROYED SOME
GREAT TREE.

WHY THE WARRIOR HAD
RUINED HIS DELICIOUS REPAST
BY PLUNGING IT INTO THE
BLIGHTING HEAT WAS QUITE BEYOND
HIM. POSSIBLY ARA WAS A FRIEND WITH WHOM
THE ARCHER WAS SHARING HIS FOOD.

BUT, TARZAN WOULD NOT RUIN GOOD
MEAT IN ANY SUCH FOOLISH MANNER ...

... SO HE GOBBLED DOWN A GREAT QUANTITY OF THE
RAW FLESH, BURYING THE BALANCE OF THE CARCASS BESIDE
THE TRAIL WHERE HE COULD FIND IT UPON HIS RETURN.

THEN TARZAN, LORD GREYSTOKE, WIPED HIS GREASY FINGERS ON HIS NAKED THIGHS AND TOOK UP KULONGA'S TRAIL. ALL DAY TARZAN FOLLOWED THE BLACK WARRIOR.

TWICE HE SAW HIM HURL HIS POISONED ARROWS OF DESTRUCTION. IN EACH INSTANCE THE ANIMAL DIED ALMOST INSTANTLY. THERE WAS SOMETHING WONDROUS IN THE TINY SLIVERS, HE THOUGHT, WHICH COULD BRING DEATH BY A MERE SCRATCH.

THAT NIGHT KULONGA SLEPT IN THE CROTCH OF A TREE, AND WHEN HE AWOKE, HIS BOW AND ARROWS HAD VANISHED. HE WAS FURIOUS-- AND FRIGHTENED. NOW HE WAS DEFENSELESS EXCEPT FOR HIS KNIFE. AND THERE WAS NO SIGN OF THE MARAUDER.

HIS ONLY HOPE LAY IN REACHING HIS FATHER'S VILLAGE AS QUICKLY AS POSSIBLE. AND IN HIS WAKE SWUNG TARZAN OF THE APES.

KULONGA'S WEAPONS WERE TIED HIGH IN THE TOP OF A TREE FROM WHICH A PATCH OF BARK HAD BEEN REMOVED NEAR TO THE GROUND, AND A HALF CUT BRANCH LEFT HANGING HIGHER UP. THUS TARZAN MARKED HIS CACHE.

HOGARTH

AS KULONGA CAME TO A CLEARING, A SLENDER COIL SPED OUT SINUOUSLY AND A QUICK NOOSE TIGHTENED ABOUT HIS NECK. HIS CRY OF ALARM WAS THROTTLED...

...AS HE SWUNG THRESHING UPWARD INTO THE LEAFY VERDURE. HAND OVER HAND TARZAN DREW HIS STRUGGLING VICTIM.

HE FASTENED THE ROPE SECURELY TO A STOUT BRANCH. THEN DESCENDING, HE PLUNGED HIS KNIFE INTO KULONGA'S HEART. KALA WAS AVENGED.

HE EXAMINED THE BLACK MINUTELY FOR HE HAD NEVER SEEN ANY OTHER HUMAN BEING. HE MARVELED AT THE TATTOOING, THE FILED TEETH; HE ADMIRED HIS DRESS AND GEAR, KNIFE AND SHEATH, AND THESE HE APPROPRIATED.

BUT NOW HE WAS HUNGRY-- AND HERE WAS MEAT, MEAT OF THE KILL.

WAS NOT KULONGA TO BE EATEN AS FAIRLY AS HORTA, THE BOAR, OR BARA, THE DEER? HE HESITATED. DID MEN EAT MEN?

ALAS, HE DID NOT KNOW--
AND THE THOUGHT STAYED HIS HAND. HE LOWERED THE BODY TO THE GROUND.

FROM A LOFTY PERCH TARZAN VIEWED THE
VILLAGE OF THATCHED HUTS ACROSS THE INTERVENING
PLANTATION. HE SAW THAT AT ONE POINT THE FOREST
TOUCHED THE VILLAGE, AND TO THIS SPOT HE MADE
HIS WAY, LURED BY A FEVER OF CURIOSITY TO BEHOLD
ANIMALS OF HIS OWN KIND, AND TO LEARN MORE OF THEIR
WAYS AND VIEW THE STRANGE LAIRS IN WHICH THEY LIVED.

HIS SAVAGE LIFE AMONG THE FIERCE, WILD BRUTES OF THE
JUNGLE LEFT NO OPENING FOR ANY THOUGHT THAT THESE
COULD BE AUGHT ELSE THAN ENEMIES. SIMILARITY OF FORM LED
HIM INTO NO ERRONEOUS CONCEPTION OF THE WELCOME
THAT WOULD BE ACCORDED HIM SHOULD HE BE DISCOVERED BY
THESE, THE FIRST OF HIS OWN KIND HE HAD EVER SEEN.

TARZAN OF THE APES WAS NO SENTIMENTALIST. HE KNEW NOTHING OF
THE BROTHERHOOD OF MAN. ALL THINGS OUTSIDE HIS OWN TRIBE
WERE HIS DEADLY ENEMIES, WITH THE FEW EXCEPTIONS OF WHICH
TANTOR, THE ELEPHANT, WAS A MARKED EXAMPLE.

AND HE REALIZED ALL THIS WITHOUT MALICE OR HATRED. TO KILL WAS THE
LAW OF THE WILD WORLD HE KNEW. FEW WERE HIS PRIMITIVE PLEASURES,
BUT THE GREATEST OF THESE WAS TO HUNT AND KILL, AND SO HE
ACCORDED TO OTHERS THE RIGHT TO CHERISH THE SAME DESIRES AS HE,
EVEN THOUGH HE HIMSELF MIGHT BE THE OBJECT OF THEIR HUNT. HIS
STRANGE LIFE HAD LEFT HIM NEITHER MOROSE NOR BLOODTHIRSTY. THAT
HE JOYED IN KILLING AND THAT HE KILLED WITH A JOYOUS LAUGH UPON
HIS HANDSOME LIPS BETOKENED NO INNATE CRUELTY. HE KILLED FOR
FOOD MOST OFTEN, BUT, BEING A MAN, HE SOMETIMES KILLED FOR
PLEASURE, A THING WHICH NO OTHER ANIMAL DOES.

AND WHEN HE KILLED FOR REVENGE, OR IN SELF-DEFENSE, HE DID THAT ALSO
WITHOUT HYSTERIA, BUT IT WAS A VERY BUSINESSLIKE PROCEEDING.

SO IT WAS THAT NOW, AS HE CAUTIOUSLY APPROACHED THE VILLAGE OF MBONGA,
HE WAS QUITE PREPARED EITHER TO KILL OR BE KILLED SHOULD HE BE DISCOVERED. HE
PROCEEDED WITH UNWONTED STEALTH, FOR KULONGA HAD TAUGHT HIM GREAT
RESPECT FOR THE LITTLE SHARP SPLINTERS OF WOOD WHICH DEALT DEATH SO SWIFTLY AND UNERRINGLY.

HOGARTH

FROM A GREAT TREE HE LOOKED
WITH WONDER UPON THIS STRANGE NEW LIFE;

HOW THE NAKED CHILDREN PLAYED; HOW THE
WOMEN WORKED AND GATHERED; AND HOW
THE MEN WERE ARMED AND GUARDED THE VILLAGE.

HE OBSERVED A WOMAN STIRRING A CAULDRON OVER A LOW FIRE. IN IT BUBBLED
A THICK, TARRY MASS. NOW AND THEN SHE DIPPED LITTLE ARROWS INTO THE SEETHING
SUBSTANCE WITH GREAT CARE. TARZAN WAS FASCINATED. THIS, HE REASONED, WAS THE DEADLY STUFF THAT KILLED.

HOW HE WISHED FOR MORE OF THESE DEADLY SLIVERS! IF ONLY THE WOMAN WOULD LEAVE HER WORK HE COULD DROP DOWN AND GATHER A HANDFUL. SUDDENLY A WILD CRY CAME FROM ACROSS THE CLEARING.

A WARRIOR, BENEATH THE VERY TREE IN WHICH HE HAD KILLED THE MURDERER OF KALA, WAS SHOUTING AND WAVING HIS SPEAR.

THE VILLAGE WAS IN AN INSTANT UPROAR. ARMED MEN RACED TO THE SCENE.

QUICKLY AND NOISELESSLY TARZAN DROPPED BESIDE THE
DESERTED CAULDRON OF POISON.
NO ONE WAS IN SIGHT.

JUST THEN THE DOORWAY OF A STRANGE HUT
CAUGHT HIS EYE. CAUTIOUSLY HE SLIPPED INSIDE.

IT WAS A ROOM FULL OF WEAPONS -- KNIVES, SHIELDS,
SPEARS ; AND ON THE FLOOR LAY A PILE OF HUMAN SKULLS.

AS HE EXAMINED EACH ARTICLE, HE REPLACED IT IN A GRUESOME FASHION.
HE CONSTRUCTED A HIDEOUS FIGURE TOPPED WITH A GRINNING SKULL, AND FASTENED A
FEATHERED HEADDRESS LIKE THE DEAD KULONGA'S. THEN HE STOOD BACK, PLEASED WITH HIS GRISLY JOKE.

BUT NOW OUTSIDE HE HEARD
THE SOUND OF WAILING. LIKE
A FLASH HE SPED OUT ...

...GATHERED UP A HANDFUL OF ARROWS, KICKED OVER
THE CAULDRON, AND LEAPED INTO THE TREES.

IN THE VILLAGE, A PROCESSION FORMED, BEARING THE BODY OF KULONGA WITH LOUD LAMENTATIONS. THEY CAME TO THE HUT WHERE TARZAN HAD BEEN, FOR THIS HAD BEEN KULONGA'S DWELLING.

M'BONGA, THE CHIEF, PEERED IN, AND QUICKLY DREW BACK. THE AWESOME DISCOVERY FILLED HIM WITH DREAD AND SUPERSTITION. FROM AFAR, TARZAN GRINNED.

KALA WAS AVENGED. TARZAN TURNED HOMEWARD TOWARD THE TRIBE OF KERCHAK, STOPPING ONLY TO RETRIEVE KULONGA'S BOW AND ARROWS FROM THE TREE TOP IN WHICH HE HAD HIDDEN THEM.

AMONGST HIS PEOPLE, TARZAN NARRATED WITH PRIDE THE GLORIES OF HIS ADVENTURE AND SHOWED THEM HIS SPOILS OF CONQUEST.

KERCHAK TURNED AWAY. SOME DAY HE WOULD WREAK HIS HATRED ON THIS UPSTART TARZAN

NOW TARZAN PRACTISED WITH HIS BOW AND ARROWS. ERE A MONTH HAD PASSED HE WAS NO MEAN SHOT; BUT LEARNING HIS SKILLS HAD COST HIM NEARLY HIS ENTIRE SUPPLY OF ARROWS. SOON HE WOULD HAVE TO REPLENISH THEM.

HE FOUND TIME TO VISIT THE CABIN, AND ONE DAY, HE CAME ON A SMALL METAL BOX. IN IT HE FOUND A PHOTOGRAPH OF A SMOOTH FACED YOUNG MAN, A GOLDEN LOCKET STUDDED WITH DIAMONDS, LINKED TO A SMALL CHAIN, A FEW LETTERS, AND A SMALL BOOK. TARZAN EXAMINED THESE ALL MINUTELY.

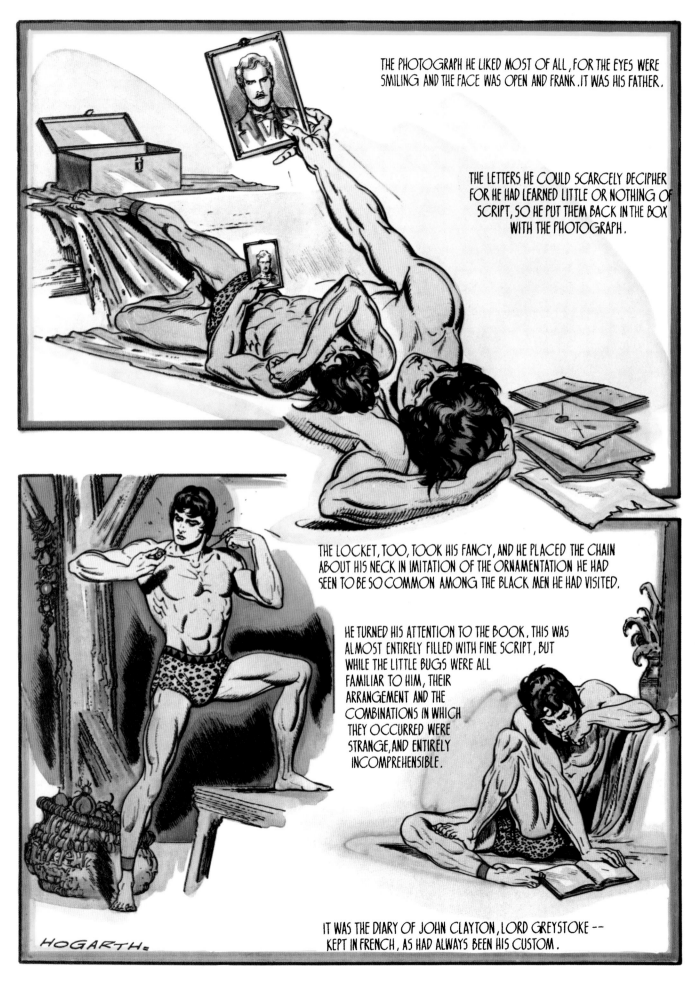

THE PHOTOGRAPH HE LIKED MOST OF ALL, FOR THE EYES WERE SMILING AND THE FACE WAS OPEN AND FRANK. IT WAS HIS FATHER.

THE LETTERS HE COULD SCARCELY DECIPHER FOR HE HAD LEARNED LITTLE OR NOTHING OF SCRIPT, SO HE PUT THEM BACK IN THE BOX WITH THE PHOTOGRAPH.

THE LOCKET, TOO, TOOK HIS FANCY, AND HE PLACED THE CHAIN ABOUT HIS NECK IN IMITATION OF THE ORNAMENTATION HE HAD SEEN TO BE SO COMMON AMONG THE BLACK MEN HE HAD VISITED.

HE TURNED HIS ATTENTION TO THE BOOK. THIS WAS ALMOST ENTIRELY FILLED WITH FINE SCRIPT, BUT WHILE THE LITTLE BUGS WERE ALL FAMILIAR TO HIM, THEIR ARRANGEMENT AND THE COMBINATIONS IN WHICH THEY OCCURRED WERE STRANGE, AND ENTIRELY INCOMPREHENSIBLE.

IT WAS THE DIARY OF JOHN CLAYTON, LORD GREYSTOKE -- KEPT IN FRENCH, AS HAD ALWAYS BEEN HIS CUSTOM.

HOGARTH

TARZAN REPLACED THE BOX IN THE CUPBOARD, BUT ALWAYS THEREAFTER HE CARRIED THE STRONG, SMILING FACE OF HIS FATHER IN HIS HEART, AND IN HIS HEAD A DETERMINATION TO SOLVE THE MYSTERY OF THE WORDS IN THE LITTLE BLACK BOOK.

AT PRESENT HE HAD MORE URGENT BUSINESS. HIS SUPPLY OF ARROWS WAS EXHAUSTED. HE RETURNED TO M'BONGA'S VILLAGE WHERE A FEAST WAS IN PREPARATION.

THE VICTIM OF THE FEAST WAS A MAN! AND AS HE WAS DRAGGED TO THE CENTER OF THE VILLAGE, THE WOMEN AND CHILDREN SET UPON HIM WITH STICKS AND STONES. TARZAN WONDERED AT THE CRUELTY OF THESE PEOPLE, AND FROM THAT MOMENT NEVER CEASED TO HOLD HIS OWN KIND IN BUT LOW ESTEEM.

NOW THEY HAD TIED THEIR POOR VICTIM TO A GREAT POST NEAR THE CENTER OF THE VILLAGE, DIRECTLY BEFORE M'BONGA'S HUT, AND HERE THEY FORMED A DANCING, YELLING CIRCLE OF WARRIORS ABOUT HIM, ALIVE WITH FLASHING KNIVES AND SPEARS.

BEYOND SQUATTED THE WOMEN, YELLING AND BEATING UPON DRUMS. IT REMINDED TARZAN OF THE DUM-DUM, AND HE KNEW WHAT TO EXPECT. HE WONDERED IF THEY WOULD SPRING UPON THEIR MEAT WHILE IT WAS STILL ALIVE. THE APES DID NOT DO SUCH THINGS AS THAT.

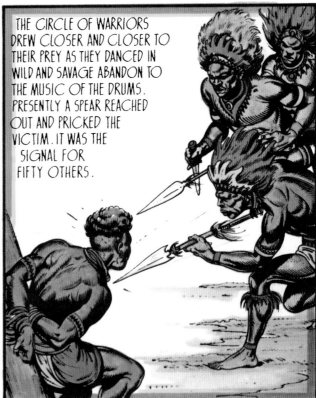

THE CIRCLE OF WARRIORS DREW CLOSER AND CLOSER TO THEIR PREY AS THEY DANCED IN WILD AND SAVAGE ABANDON TO THE MUSIC OF THE DRUMS. PRESENTLY A SPEAR REACHED OUT AND PRICKED THE VICTIM. IT WAS THE SIGNAL FOR FIFTY OTHERS.

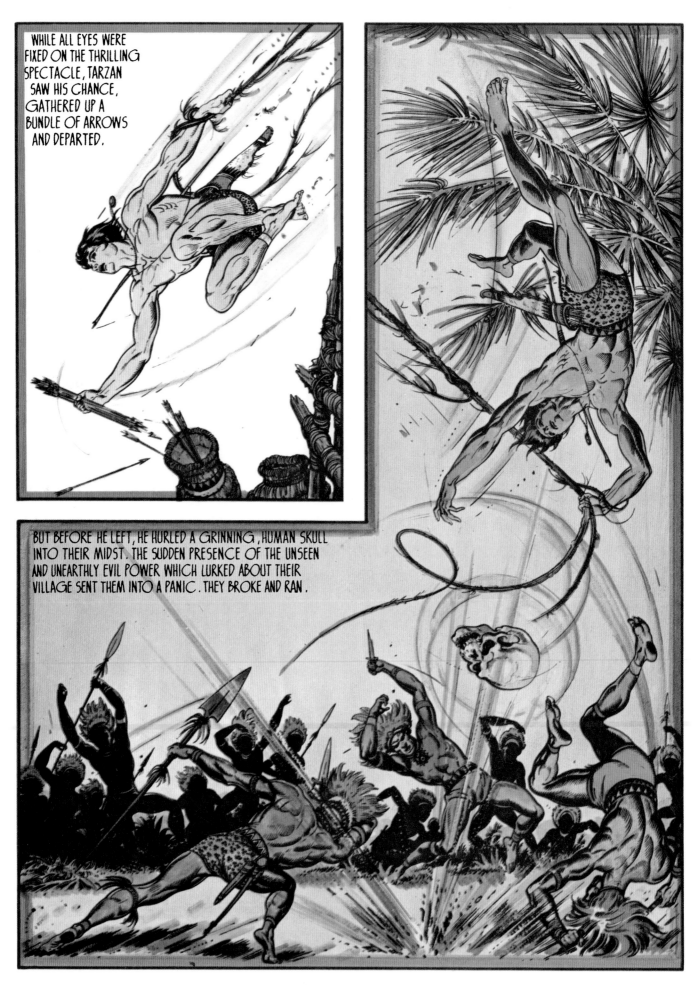

WHILE ALL EYES WERE FIXED ON THE THRILLING SPECTACLE, TARZAN SAW HIS CHANCE, GATHERED UP A BUNDLE OF ARROWS AND DEPARTED.

BUT BEFORE HE LEFT, HE HURLED A GRINNING, HUMAN SKULL INTO THEIR MIDST. THE SUDDEN PRESENCE OF THE UNSEEN AND UNEARTHLY EVIL POWER WHICH LURKED ABOUT THEIR VILLAGE SENT THEM INTO A PANIC. THEY BROKE AND RAN.

TARZAN OF THE APES HUNTED AS HE TRAVELED HOMEWARD.

SUDDENLY HE SAW SABOR NOT TWENTY PACES AWAY. THE LIONESS CROUCHED, YELLOW EYES GLEAMING.

TARZAN DID NOT ATTEMPT TO ESCAPE. IN FACT HE WELCOMED THE OPPORTUNITY TO TEST HIS NEW SKILL. QUICKLY HE UN-SLUNG HIS BOW AND FITTED A WELL-DAUBED ARROW.

AS HE DREW THE TAUT BOWSTRING, THE GREAT CAT SPRANG. THE SLIVERED MISSILE LEAPED TO MEET HER IN MID-AIR.

AS QUICKLY AS SABOR HIT THE GROUND, TARZAN WHIRLED AND SANK ANOTHER SHAFT, AND A THIRD...

...LIGHTNINGLIKE, STRUCK HER FULL IN AN EYE.

IN A SCREAMING RAGE THE ONRUSHING BODY BORE HIM DOWN; BUT EVEN AS HE FELL, HIS POWERFUL KNIFE STRUCK AGAIN AND AGAIN BEFORE HE REALIZED HIS MIGHTY ADVERSARY WAS DEAD.

A WAVE OF EXULTATION SWEPT OVER TARZAN OF THE APES.

HE GAZED AT HIS ENEMY. NEVER HAD HE SEEN SABOR SO INERT AND STILL.

NOW TRULY DID HE FEEL THE POWER OF HIS FORCE AND SKILL. HE PLACED A FOOT UPON HIS POWERFUL ENEMY, AND THROWING BACK HIS HEAD, ROARED OUT THE AWFUL CHALLENGE OF THE VICTORIOUS BULL APE.

FIRST HE THOUGHT TO REMOVE THE HIDE. RITUALLY HE
ATE OF THE TOUGH, UNSAVORY MEAT OUT OF RESPECT FOR
SABOR. REFRESHED, HE CONTINUED HIS PROGRESS TOWARD THE DOMAIN OF THE APE TRIBE.

WHEN HE FOUND THEM, HE TOLD
OF HIS GREAT EXPLOIT. NOW PROUDLY
HE EXHIBITED HIS TROPHY, THE PELT
OF SABOR, THE LIONESS.

THE TRIBE GATHERED TO LOOK UPON THE PROOF OF HIS WONDROUS PROWESS. ONLY KERCHAK HUNG BACK NURSING HIS HATRED AND RAGE. SUDDENLY SOMETHING SNAPPED IN THE WICKED LITTLE BRAIN OF THE ANTHROPOID.

WITH A FRIGHTFUL ROAR THE GREAT BEAST SPRANG AMONG THE ASSEMBLAGE.

BITING AND STRIKING, HE KILLED AND MAIMED A DOZEN ERE THE BALANCE COULD ESCAPE HIS WRATH.

FROTHING AND SHRIEKING, KERCHAK SAW THE OBJECT OF HIS HATRED ON A NEARBY LIMB. "COME DOWN, TARZAN, GREAT KILLER. COME DOWN AND FEEL THE FANGS OF A GREATER!"

AS THE TRIBE WATCHED BREATHLESSLY, TARZAN QUIETLY DROPPED TO THE GROUND.

NEARLY SEVEN FEET STOOD KERCHAK ON HIS SHORT LEGS. HIS LIPS EXPOSED GREAT FANGS AND HIS EYES SHOT GLEAMS OF MADNESS. AWAITING HIM STOOD TARZAN, ARMED ONLY WITH HIS KNIFE AND HIS SUPERIOR INTELLECT TO OFFSET THE FEROCIOUS STRENGTH OF HIS ENEMY.

AS THE BRUTE CAME ROARING AT HIM, TARZAN MOVED TO MEET THE ATTACK. WARDING OFF THE ENCIRCLING ARMS---

---HE DODGED, SPRANG IN, AND DROVE THE KNIFE TO THE HILT INTO KERCHAK'S BODY.

BEFORE HE COULD WRENCH THE BLADE FREE AGAIN, THE BULL'S QUICK LUNGE TO SEIZE HIM IN THOSE AWFUL ARMS...

... HAD TORN THE WEAPON FROM TARZAN'S GRASP.

KERCHAK AIMED A TERRIFIC BLOW AT THE APE-MAN'S HEAD WITH THE FLAT OF HIS HAND, A BLOW WHICH, HAD IT LANDED, MIGHT EASILY HAVE CRUSHED IN THE SIDE OF TARZAN'S SKULL.

THE MAN WAS TOO QUICK, AND, DUCKING BENEATH IT, HIMSELF DELIVERED A MIGHTY ONE, WITH CLENCHED FIST, IN THE PIT OF KERCHAK'S STOMACH.

THE APE WAS STAGGERED. DESPITE THE MORTAL WOUND IN HIS SIDE, HE RALLIED IN ONE MIGHTY EFFORT. HE CLOSED UPON THE APE-MAN AND THE GREAT JAWS SOUGHT TARZAN'S THROAT.

BUT THE YOUNG LORD'S SINEWY FINGERS WERE AT KERCHAK'S OWN THROAT BEFORE THE CRUEL FANGS COULD CLOSE ON TARZAN'S SLEEK BROWN SKIN.

THUS THEY STRUGGLED, THE ONE TO CRUSH OUT HIS OPPONENT'S LIFE WITH THOSE AWFUL TEETH, THE OTHER TO CLOSE FOREVER THE WINDPIPE BENEATH HIS GRASP. FOR A WHILE, TARZAN HELD THE SNARLING JAWS FROM HIM. THE GREATER STRENGTH OF THE APE WAS SLOWLY PREVAILING, AND THE FANGS OF THE BEAST WERE CLOSE UPON TARZAN'S THROAT WHEN...

...WITH A SHUDDERING TREMOR, THE GREAT APE STIFFENED FOR AN INSTANT AND THEN SANK LIMPLY TO THE GROUND. KERCHAK WAS DEAD.

WITHDRAWING THE
KNIFE THAT HAD SO OFTEN
RENDERED HIM MASTER OF
FAR MIGHTIER MUSCLES
THAN HIS OWN, TARZAN OF
THE APES PLACED HIS FOOT
UPON THE NECK OF HIS
VANQUISHED ENEMY, AND ONCE
AGAIN, LOUD THROUGH THE FOREST RANG
THE FIERCE, WILD CRY OF CONQUEROR.

HOGARTH.

JUNGLE TALES OF
Tarzan

Edgar Rice Burroughs

BY
BURNE
HOGARTH

ALL NEW !

DEDICATION

To my mother:

She worked all her life, hard and heroically,
the wife and mother of a worker's family; but
never did she lose the appreciation of rare
good things. Even in dire times, the twinkling
eye, the smile, the flash of keen enjoyment of
humor and fantasy were marvelous to behold
—and are wonderful to recall. This book, I
am sure, would have been for her a moment
of pure joy.

—Burne Hogarth, 1976

JUNGLE TALES OF Tarzan

BOOK ONE

Tarzan's first love

TEEKA, STRETCHED AT LUXURIOUS EASE IN THE SHADE OF THE TROPICAL FOREST, PRESENTED, UNQUESTIONABLY, A MOST ALLURING PICTURE OF YOUNG, FEMININE LOVELINESS. OR AT LEAST SO THOUGHT TARZAN OF THE APES, WHO SQUATTED UPON A LOW-SWINGING BRANCH IN A NEARBY TREE AND LOOKED DOWN UPON HER.

HOGARTH

JUST TO HAVE SEEN HIM THERE, LOLLING UPON THE SWAYING BOUGH, HIS BROWN SKIN MOTTLED BY THE BRILLIANT EQUATORIAL SUNLIGHT WHICH PERCOLATED THROUGH THE LEAFY CANOPY OF GREEN ABOVE HIM, HIS CLEAN-LIMBED BODY RELAXED IN GRACEFUL EASE, HIS SHAPELY HEAD PARTLY TURNED IN CONTEMPLATIVE ABSORPTION, AND HIS INTELLIGENT, GRAY EYES DREAMILY DEVOURING THE OBJECT OF THEIR DEVOTION, YOU WOULD HAVE THOUGHT HIM THE REINCARNATION OF SOME DEMIGOD OF OLD.

YOU WOULD NOT HAVE GUESSED THAT IN INFANCY HE HAD SUCKLED AT THE BREAST OF A HAIRY SHE-APE, NOR THAT IN ALL HIS CONSCIOUS PAST, SINCE HIS PARENTS HAD PASSED AWAY IN THE LITTLE CABIN BY THE HARBOR AT THE JUNGLE'S VERGE, HE HAD KNOWN NO OTHER ASSOCIATES THAN THE SULLEN BULLS AND THE SNARLING COWS OF THE TRIBE OF KERCHAK, THE GREAT APE.

NOR, COULD YOU HAVE READ THE THOUGHTS WHICH PASSED THROUGH THAT ACTIVE, HEALTHY BRAIN, THE DESIRES AND ASPIRATIONS WHICH THE SIGHT OF TEEKA INSPIRED, WOULD YOU HAVE BEEN ANY MORE INCLINED TO GIVE CREDENCE TO THE REALITY OF THE ORIGIN OF THE APE-MAN. FOR, FROM HIS THOUGHTS ALONE, YOU COULD NEVER HAVE GLEANED THE TRUTH -- THAT HE HAD BEEN BORN TO A GENTLE ENGLISH LADY OR THAT HIS SIRE HAD BEEN AN ENGLISH NOBLEMAN OF TIME-HONORED LINEAGE. LOST TO TARZAN OF THE APES WAS THE TRUTH OF HIS ORIGIN. THAT HE WAS JOHN CLAYTON, LORD GREYSTOKE, WITH A SEAT IN THE HOUSE OF LORDS, HE DID NOT KNOW, NOR, KNOWING, WOULD HAVE UNDERSTOOD.

YES, TEEKA WAS INDEED BEAUTIFUL! OF COURSE KALA HAD BEEN BEAUTIFUL -- ONE'S MOTHER IS ALWAYS THAT -- BUT TEEKA WAS BEAUTIFUL IN A WAY ALL HER OWN, AN INDESCRIBABLE SORT OF WAY ...

... WHICH TARZAN WAS JUST BEGINNING TO SENSE IN A RATHER VAGUE AND HAZY MANNER. HE ENVIED HER THE HANDSOME COAT OF HAIR WHICH COVERED HER BODY. HIS OWN SMOOTH, BROWN HIDE HE HATED WITH A HATRED BORN OF DISGUST AND CONTEMPT.

THEN THERE WERE TEEKA'S GREAT TEETH, NOT SO LARGE AS THE MALE'S, OF COURSE, BUT STILL MIGHTY, HANDSOME THINGS BY COMPARISON WITH TARZAN'S FEEBLE WHITE ONES. AND HER BEETLING BROWS, HER BROAD, FLAT NOSE, AND HER MOUTH! TARZAN HAD OFTEN PRACTICED MAKING HIS MOUTH INTO A LITTLE CIRCLE ...

... AND THEN PUFFING OUT HIS CHEEKS WHILE HE WINKED HIS EYES RAPIDLY; BUT HE FELT HE COULD NEVER DO IT IN THE SAME CUTE AND IRRESISTIBLE WAY IN WHICH TEEKA DID IT.

AND AS TARZAN
WATCHED HER
THAT AFTER-
NOON AND
WONDERED ...

... A YOUNG BULL APE, WHO HAD BEEN
LAZILY FORAGING FOR FOOD BENEATH THE
DAMP, MATTED CARPET OF DECAYING VEGETATION
AT THE ROOTS OF A NEAR-BY TREE, LUMBERED
AWKWARDLY IN TEEKA'S DIRECTION .

TARZAN HAD ALWAYS LIKED TAUG . WHY, THEN,
SHOULD TARZAN FEEL THE RISE OF THE SHORT
HAIRS AT THE NAPE OF HIS NECK MERELY
BECAUSE TAUG SAT CLOSE TO TEEKA ?

FOR A FEW MINUTES, THE YOUNG APE-MAN WATCHED TAUG PRESS CLOSER TO TEEKA. HE SAW THE ROUGH CARESS OF THE HUGE PAW AS IT STROKED THE SLEEK SHOULDER OF THE SHE...

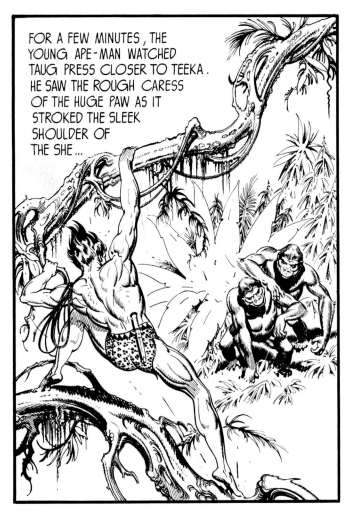

... AND THEN TARZAN OF THE APES SLIPPED CATLIKE TO THE GROUND AND APPROACHED THE TWO.

"TEEKA IS TARZAN'S," SAID THE APE-MAN IN THE LOW GUTTURALS OF THE GREAT ANTHROPOIDS. "TEEKA IS TAUG'S," REPLIED THE BULL APE.

HOGARTH

TAUG MADE A SUDDEN LUNGE FOR TARZAN, BUT THE APE-MAN LEAPED NIMBLY TO ONE SIDE.

TARZAN REACHED FOR HIS KNIFE ...

... AND AIMED A VICIOUS BLOW AT TAUG'S NECK. BUT THE APE WHEELED AND THE KEEN BLADE STRUCK HIM BUT A GLANCING BLOW UPON THE SHOULDER.

A SPURT OF RED BLOOD GUSHED FORTH ...

... AND IT BROUGHT A SHRILL CRY OF DELIGHT FROM TEEKA.

IF TEEKA HAD NOT BEEN SO ABSORBED, SHE MIGHT HAVE NOTED THE RUSTLING OF THE LEAVES IN THE TREE ABOVE HER -- A RUSTLING WHICH WAS NOT CAUSED BY ANY MOVEMENT OF THE WIND, SINCE THERE WAS NO WIND.

AND HAD TEEKA LOOKED UP, SHE MIGHT HAVE SEEN A SLEEK BODY CROUCHING ALMOST DIRECTLY OVER HER AND WICKED YELLOW EYES GLARING HUNGRILY DOWN UPON HER. BUT TEEKA DID NOT LOOK UP.

TAUG HAD HALTED NOW AND WAS PREPARING TO MAKE A NEW STAND. HIS LIPS WERE FLECKED WITH FOAM AND SALIVA DROOLED FROM HIS JOWLS.

IT WAS DURING THIS PAUSE THAT TAUG CHANCED TO LET HIS EYES ROVE BEYOND HIS FOEMAN. INSTANTLY THE ENTIRE ASPECT OF THE APE ALTERED. RAGE LEFT HIS COUNTENANCE TO BE SUPPLANTED BY AN EXPRESSION OF FEAR.

WITH A CRY THAT TARZAN RECOGNIZED WELL, TAUG TURNED AND FLED. NO NEED TO QUESTION HIM -- HIS WARNING PROCLAIMED THE NEAR PRESENCE OF THEIR ANCIENT ENEMY.

TARZAN STARTED TO SEEK SAFETY, AND AS HE DID SO HE HEARD A PANTHER'S SCREAM MINGLED WITH THE FRIGHTENED CRY OF A SHE-APE.

TAUG HEARD TOO; BUT HE DID NOT PAUSE IN HIS FLIGHT.

WITH THE APE-MAN, HOWEVER, IT WAS DIFFERENT. HE LOOKED BACK, AND THE SIGHT THAT MET HIS EYES FILLED HIM WITH HORROR.

TARZAN SAW THAT TEEKA MUST DIE.

TARZAN RACED TO INTERCEPT THE BEAST, TAKING DOWN HIS ROPE AS HE RAN. HE WAS NOT FAR BEHIND, BUT HE COULD NOT OVERHAUL THE BRUTE BEFORE IT REACHED TEEKA. HE MUST CHANCE A LONG THROW.

SHEETA SPRANG FOR TEEKA JUST AS THE APE LEAPED FOR THE LOWER LIMB OF A TREE.

BUT NOW THE COILS OF A GRASS ROPE CLEAVED THE AIR AND SETTLED ON THE SAVAGE HEAD.

THE NOOSE CLOSED AND THE ROPE SNAPPED SHUT.

TARZAN BRACED AND THE BIG BEAST WHIRLED AND FELL ON ITS BACK.

INSTANTLY SHEETA WAS UP, BELLOWING HIDEOUS CRIES OF RAGE.

TEEKA WAS SAFE -- BUT NOW TARZAN FACED THE ENRAGED CAT'S MURDEROUS CHARGE.

SHEETA ARCHED IN A POWERFUL LEAP. TARZAN
PIVOTED TO ONE SIDE AND THE PANTHER WENT
HURTLING TO THE GROUND BEYOND. AS SHEETA
RECOVERED, TARZAN RACED FOR SAFETY.

DRAGGING THE APE-MAN'S
ROPE BEHIND, THE BEAST
DOUBLED BACK AND
TORE AFTER
HIS PREY.

HE CIRCLED
A LOW BUSH,
BECAME
ENTANGLED...

...AND WAS
BROUGHT TO
A SUDDEN
STOP. AN
INSTANT LATER,

TARZAN WAS SAFE IN THE BRANCHES OF A TREE.

HERE HE PERCHED, HURLING
TWIGS AT THE RAGING
FELINE. SHEETA, GOADED
TO FRENZY, SNAPPED
THE GRASS ROPE, AND
WITH A FINAL SCREAM
OF RAGE, HE SLUNK
OFF INTO THE
TANGLED MAZES
OF THE
JUNGLE.

AN HOUR LATER, WHILE TARZAN WAS FASHIONING A NEW NOOSE, TEEKA CAME AND SQUATTED BESIDE HIM. TAUG EYED THEM SULLENLY, BUT HE DID NOT PROVOKE A QUARREL.

WITH HIS ROPE REPAIRED, TARZAN TOOK TO THE TREES IN SEARCH OF GAME. TAUG SAW HIM DEPART, AND QUITE CASUALLY THE BIG BULL CAME CLOSE TO TEEKA. THERE WAS NO EVIDENCE OF ANGER ON HER FACE.

TAUG EXPANDED HIS CHEST, BEAT A SHORT TATTOO, AND MADE STRANGE GROWLINGS.

TEEKA LET HER EYES REST IN ADMIRATION ON THE POWERFUL TAUG. WHAT A BEAUTIFUL CREATURE HE WAS INDEED!

WHEN TARZAN RETURNED FROM HUNTING, TEEKA WAS CONTENTEDLY SCRATCHING THE BACK OF HIS RIVAL. TARZAN WAS DISGUSTED. WITH A GRIMACE, HE TURNED AWAY FROM THE CAUSE OF HIS HEARTACHE.

THE APE-MAN CRAVED AFFECTION. FROM BABY-HOOD UNTIL THE TIME WHEN KULONGA'S POISONED ARROW...

TARZAN WAS SUFFERING THE FIRST PANGS OF BLIGHTED LOVE.

...TOOK HIS SAVAGE FOSTER-MOTHER FROM HIM, KALA REPRESENTED TO TARZAN THE SOLE OBJECT OF LOVE WHICH HE HAD KNOWN. IN TEEKA, HE HAD SEEN WITHIN THE PAST FEW HOURS A SUBSTITUTE FOR KALA -- SOMEONE TO FIGHT FOR AND TO HUNT FOR -- SOMEONE TO CARESS; BUT NOW HIS DREAM WAS SHATTERED.

TARZAN SHOOK HIS HEAD AND GROWLED; THEN ON AND ON THROUGH THE JUNGLE HE SWUNG.

AND ONCE TARZAN HALTED, SIGHING, TO WATCH NUMA, THE LION, AND SABOR, THE LIONESS, PASS BENEATH HIM.

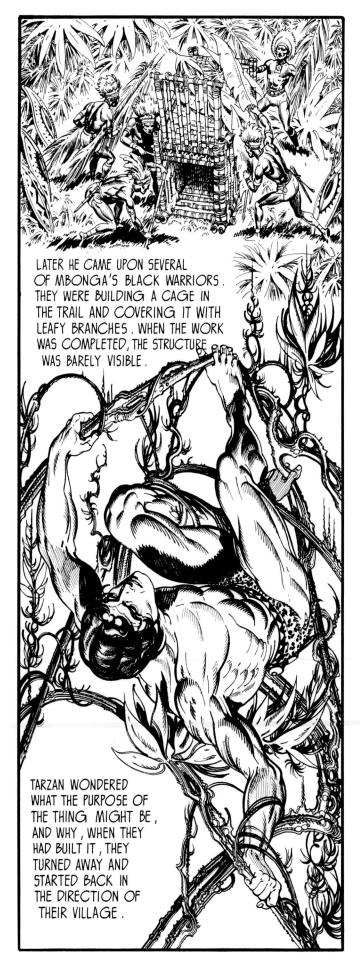

LATER HE CAME UPON SEVERAL
OF MBONGA'S BLACK WARRIORS.
THEY WERE BUILDING A CAGE IN
THE TRAIL AND COVERING IT WITH
LEAFY BRANCHES. WHEN THE WORK
WAS COMPLETED, THE STRUCTURE
WAS BARELY VISIBLE.

TARZAN WONDERED
WHAT THE PURPOSE OF
THE THING MIGHT BE,
AND WHY, WHEN THEY
HAD BUILT IT, THEY
TURNED AWAY AND
STARTED BACK IN
THE DIRECTION OF
THEIR VILLAGE.

HOGARTH=

AS THEY MOVED ALONG THE TRAIL,
TARZAN FOLLOWED IN THEIR WAKE.

IT HAD BEEN SOME TIME
SINCE HE HAD VISITED THE BLACKS
FROM AMONG WHOM HAD COME
KULONGA, THE SLAYER OF KALA. FROM THE
CONCEALMENT OF HIS TREE ABOVE THE PALISADE...

...TARZAN SAW VILLAGERS DISCUSSING
EVENTS OF THE DAY... AND IN THE DARKER
CORNERS HE DESCRIED ISOLATED COUPLES
LAUGHING AND TALKING TOGETHER.

TARZAN WENT
TO SLEEP THAT
NIGHT WITH VISIONS
OF TEEKA FILLING
HIS DREAMS...

...SHE AND TARZAN, LAUGHING AND TALKING
LIKE THE YOUNG BLACK MEN AND WOMEN.

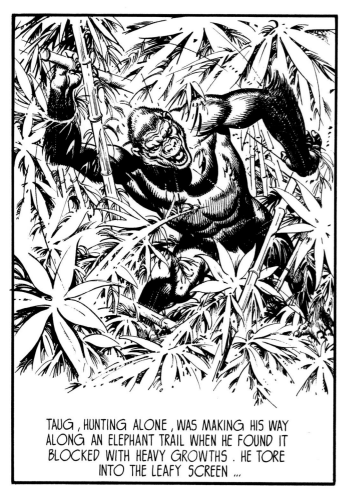

TAUG, HUNTING ALONE, WAS MAKING HIS WAY ALONG AN ELEPHANT TRAIL WHEN HE FOUND IT BLOCKED WITH HEAVY GROWTHS. HE TORE INTO THE LEAFY SCREEN ...

...AND FOUND HIMSELF WITHIN A STRANGE LAIR, HIS PROGRESS EFFECTUALLY BLOCKED. BITING AND STRIKING AT THE BARRIER WITHOUT RESULT, TAUG TURNED TO RETREAT ...

...ONLY TO FIND THAT ANOTHER BARRIER HAD DROPPED BEHIND HIM. TAUG WAS TRAPPED. IN A FRIGHTFUL RAGE, HE FOUGHT FRANTICALLY FOR HIS FREEDOM.

IN THE MORNING ,
A PARTY OF BLACKS SET OUT FROM THE VILLAGE IN THE
DIRECTION OF THE TRAP, WHILE AMONG THE BRANCHES
OF THE TREES ABOVE THEM HOVERED A NAKED WHITE
GIANT, FILLED WITH THE CURIOSITY OF THE WILD THINGS .

WHEN THE BLACKS
REACHED THE TRAP,
TAUG SET UP A
GREAT COMMOTION.

SEIZING THE BARS OF HIS PRISON , HE SHOOK THEM FRANTICALLY, AND ALL THE WHILE HE
ROARED AND GROWLED TERRIBLY . THE BLACKS WERE ELATED, FOR WHILE THEY HAD NOT
BUILT THEIR TRAP FOR THIS HAIRY TREE MAN , THEY WERE DELIGHTED WITH THEIR CATCH .

NOR WAS IT LONG BEFORE THERE CAME THE FAMILIAR ODOR THAT TOLD HIM THE IDENTITY OF THE CAPTIVE AS UNERRINGLY AS THOUGH HE LOOKED UPON TAUG WITH HIS EYES. YES, IT WAS TAUG, AND HE WAS ALONE.

TARZAN PRICKED UP HIS EARS WHEN HE HEARD THE VOICE OF A GREAT APE AND, CIRCLING QUICKLY UNTIL HE WAS DOWN WIND FROM THE TRAP, HE SNIFFED THE AIR FOR THE SCENT SPOOR OF THE PRISONER.

TARZAN GRINNED. HE SAW THE WARRIORS STRIP THE SCREEN FROM ABOUT THE CAGE, FASTEN ROPES TO IT, AND DRAG IT AWAY IN THE DIRECTION OF THEIR VILLAGE.

TARZAN APPROACHED TO SEE WHAT THE BLACKS WOULD DO WITH THEIR PRISONER. DOUBTLESS THEY WOULD SLAY HIM. NOW HE COULD HAVE TEEKA, WITH NONE TO DISPUTE HIS RIGHT TO HER.

TARZAN WATCHED UNTIL HIS RIVAL PASSED OUT OF SIGHT, STILL BEATING ON THE BARS OF HIS PRISON AND GROWLING OUT HIS ANGER AND HIS THREATS.

THEN THE APE-MAN TURNED AND SWUNG RAPIDLY OFF IN SEARCH OF THE TRIBE, AND TEEKA.

ONCE UPON THE JOURNEY, HE SURPRISED SHEETA AND HIS FAMILY IN A CLEARING. THE GREAT CAT LAY UPON THE GROUND, WHILE HIS MATE LICKED AT THE SOFT WHITE FUR AT HIS THROAT.

BEFORE LONG, HE CAME TO THE CLEARING. TEEKA WAS FEEDING BY HERSELF.

NOT FOR LONG WOULD SHE FEED IN LONE-LINESS, HE THOUGHT AS HE SWUNG DOWN.

"TEEKA," HE CALLED OUT, "IT IS TARZAN. I HAVE COME FOR YOU. YOU BELONG TO TARZAN." THE SHE-APE DREW AWAY. "WHERE IS TAUG," SHE ASKED SUSPICIOUSLY.

"THE GOMANGANI HAVE HIM," REPLIED TARZAN. "THEY WILL KILL HIM." IN THE EYES OF THE SHE, TARZAN SAW A WISTFUL EXPRESSION.

BUT SHE CAME QUITE CLOSE AND SNUGGLED AGAINST HIM, AND TARZAN, LORD GREYSTOKE, PUT HIS ARM ABOUT HER ...

...BUT AS HE DID SO, HE NOTICED, WITH A START, THAT STRANGE INCONGRUITY OF HIS SMOOTH, BROWN ARM AGAINST THE BLACK AND HAIRY COAT OF HIS BELOVED.

HE RECALLED THE PAW OF SHEETA'S MATE ACROSS SHEETA'S FACE -- NO INCONGRUITY THERE. HE THOUGHT OF LITTLE MANU HUGGING HIS SHE, AND HOW ONE SEEMED TO BELONG TO THE OTHER. EVEN THE PROUD MALE BIRD, WITH HIS GAY PLUMAGE, BORE A RESEMBLANCE TO HIS QUIETER SPOUSE.

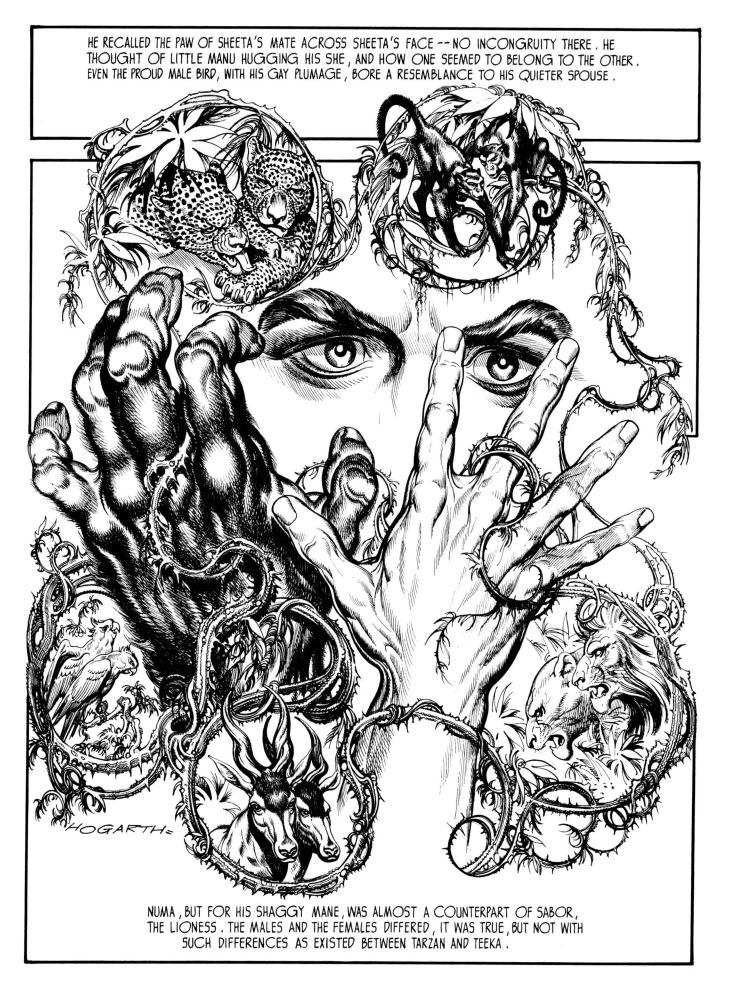

NUMA, BUT FOR HIS SHAGGY MANE, WAS ALMOST A COUNTERPART OF SABOR, THE LIONESS. THE MALES AND THE FEMALES DIFFERED, IT WAS TRUE, BUT NOT WITH SUCH DIFFERENCES AS EXISTED BETWEEN TARZAN AND TEEKA.

TARZAN WAS PUZZLED. THERE WAS SOMETHING WRONG.

HIS ARM DROPPED FROM THE SHOULDER OF TEEKA. VERY SLOWLY, HE DREW AWAY FROM HER.

SHE LOOKED AT HIM WITH HER HEAD COCKED TO ONE SIDE.

AS SHE WATCHED HIM, SHE SAW HIM SWING INTO A NEARBY TREE AND DISAPPEAR FROM SIGHT.

MBONGA'S WARRIORS, TOILING BENEATH THEIR STRENUOUS TASK OF MOVING THE SAVAGE APE IN THE PRIMITIVE CAGE, MADE SLOW PROGRESS TOWARD THEIR VILLAGE.

IN THE TREES, TARZAN WATCHED THE BLACKS. THEY WERE EXHAUSTED. ALREADY SEVERAL OF THEM SLEPT. PRESENTLY, ONLY ONE OF THE WARRIORS WAS STILL AWAKE.

THE MAN AROSE AND MOVED TO THE REAR OF THE CAGE TO EXAMINE ITS FASTENINGS. TAUG EYED THE WARRIOR AND EMITTED LOW GROWLS.

IN A WHISPER INAUDIBLE TO THE WARRIOR, TARZAN CAUTIONED THE APE TO SILENCE, AND TAUG'S GROWLING CEASED.

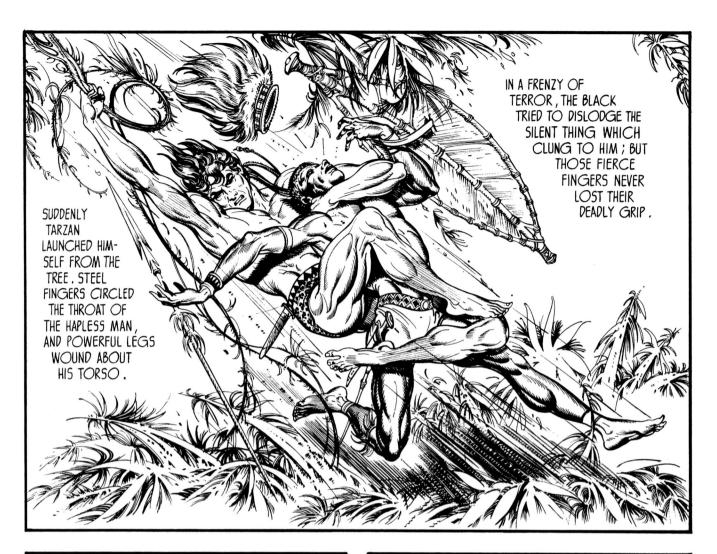

SUDDENLY TARZAN LAUNCHED HIMSELF FROM THE TREE. STEEL FINGERS CIRCLED THE THROAT OF THE HAPLESS MAN, AND POWERFUL LEGS WOUND ABOUT HIS TORSO.

IN A FRENZY OF TERROR, THE BLACK TRIED TO DISLODGE THE SILENT THING WHICH CLUNG TO HIM; BUT THOSE FIERCE FINGERS NEVER LOST THEIR DEADLY GRIP.

TAUG WAS A SILENT WITNESS TO THE RELENTLESS STRUGGLE. NOW HE SAW THE GOMANGANI SUDDENLY GO LIMP.

TARZAN SPRANG TO THE DOOR OF THE CAGE ...

... WORKED RAPIDLY AT THE THONGS. HE LIFTED THE BARRIER AND TAUG CRAWLED OUT.

THE APE WOULD
HAVE TURNED UPON
THE SLEEPING BLACKS THAT HE
MIGHT WRECK HIS PENT VENGEANCE;
BUT TARZAN WOULD NOT PERMIT IT.

INSTEAD, TARZAN AND TAUG TOOK TO THE TREES
TOGETHER, THE SHAGGY COAT OF THE FIERCE APE
BRUSHING THE SLEEK SKIN OF THE ENGLISH LORDLING AS
THEY PASSED THROUGH THE PRIMEVAL JUNGLE SIDE BY SIDE.

AT LAST THEY NEARED THE PRECINCTS OF THE TRIBE.
"GO BACK TO TEEKA," SAID TARZAN. "SHE IS
YOURS. TARZAN DOES NOT WANT HER."

"TARZAN HAS FOUND ANOTHER SHE?" ASKED TAUG.

THE APE-MAN REGARDED THE APE, THEN GAZED TO THE FAR HORIZON.

HOGARTH.

"FOR THE GOMANGANI THERE IS ANOTHER
GOMANGANI," HE SAID; "FOR NUMA, THE LION, THERE IS SABOR,
THE LIONESS; FOR SHEETA THERE IS A SHE OF HIS OWN KIND; FOR
BARA, THE DEER; FOR MANU, THE MONKEY; FOR ALL THE BEASTS AND THE BIRDS OF
THE JUNGLE THERE IS A MATE. ONLY FOR TARZAN OF THE APES IS THERE NONE. TAUG IS AN APE.
TEEKA IS AN APE. GO BACK TO TEEKA. TARZAN IS A MAN. HE WILL GO ALONE."

The CAPTURE of Tarzan

BOOK TWO

THE BLACK WARRIORS LABORED
IN THE HUMID HEAT OF THE JUNGLE'S
STIFLING SHADE . WITH WAR SPEARS THEY
LOOSENED THE THICK , BLACK LOAM AND THE
DEEP LAYERS OF ROTTING VEGETATION . WITH
HEAVY-NAILED FINGERS THEY SCOOPED AWAY
THE DISINTEGRATED EARTH FROM THE CENTER
OF THE AGE-OLD GAME TRAIL .

OFTEN THEY CEASED THEIR LABORS TO SQUAT, RESTING AND GOSSIPING, WITH MUCH LAUGHTER, AT THE EDGE OF THE PIT THEY WERE DIGGING.

SWEAT GLISTENED ON THEIR SMOOTH, EBON SKINS, BENEATH WHICH ROLLED ROUNDED MUSCLES, SUPPLE IN THE PERFECTION OF NATURE'S UNCONTAMINATED HEALTH.

ABOVE THEM, A GRAY-EYED GIANT WATCHED WITH EAGER INTENTNESS THEIR EVERY MOVE.

EVIDENT WAS THE WATCHER'S DESIRE TO KNOW THE PURPOSE OF THE BLACK MEN'S LABORS. SUCH
A ONE AS THESE IT WAS WHO HAD SLAIN HIS BELOVED KALA, YET HE LIKED WELL TO WATCH THEM,
AVID AS HE WAS FOR GREATER KNOWLEDGE OF THE WAYS OF MAN.

HE SAW THE PIT GROW IN DEPTH UNTIL A GREAT HOLE YAWNED THE WIDTH OF THE TRAIL.
TARZAN COULD NOT GUESS THE PURPOSE OF SO GREAT A LABOR.

AND WHEN THEY CUT LONG STAKES, SHARPENED AT THEIR UPPER ENDS, AND SET THEM AT INTERVALS UPRIGHT IN THE BOTTOM OF THE PIT, HIS WONDERMENT BUT INCREASED...

...NOR WAS IT SATISFIED WITH THE PLACING OF THE LIGHT CROSS-POLES OVER THE PIT...

...OR THE CAREFUL ARRANGEMENT OF LEAVES AND EARTH WHICH COMPLETELY HID FROM VIEW THE WORK THE BLACK MEN HAD PERFORMED.

WHEN THEY WERE DONE, THEY SURVEYED THEIR WORK WITH SATISFACTION. EVEN TO TARZAN'S PRACTICED EYE, THERE REMAINED LITTLE EVIDENCE THAT THE GAME TRAIL HAD BEEN TAMPERED WITH IN ANY WAY.

SHORTLY AFTER THE BLACKS HAD DEPARTED, TARZAN SWUNG DOWN TO THE TRAIL. SNIFFING SUSPICIOUSLY, HE SCRAPED AWAY THE EARTH TO EXPOSE THE CROSS-BARS AND THE PIT.

HE STUDIED IT, THEN CAREFULLY REARRANGED THE WORK AS HE HAD FOUND IT.

THIS DONE, HE SWUNG AWAY IN SEARCH OF THE TRIBE OF KERCHAK. TARZAN COULD NOT GUESS THE PURPOSE OF THE COVERED PIT, FOR THE WAYS OF THE BLACKS WERE STILL STRANGE TO HIM.

ALONG THE WAY, A SHIFTING WIND BROUGHT TO HIS KEEN NOSTRILS A FAMILIAR, PUNGENT ODOR CLOSE AT HAND, AND A MOMENT LATER THERE LOOMED BENEATH HIM A HUGE, GRAY-BLACK BULK, FORGING STEADILY ALONG THE TRAIL.

TARZAN SEIZED AND BROKE A SMALL TREE LIMB, AND AT THE SUDDEN CRACKING SOUND, THE PONDEROUS FIGURE HALTED.

GREAT EARS WERE THROWN FORWARD, AND A LONG, SUPPLE TRUNK ROSE QUICKLY TO WAVE TO AND FRO IN SEARCH OF THE SCENT OF AN ENEMY...

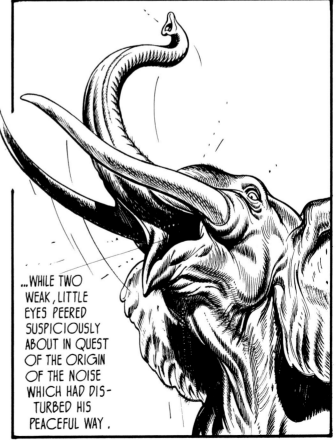

...WHILE TWO WEAK, LITTLE EYES PEERED SUSPICIOUSLY ABOUT IN QUEST OF THE ORIGIN OF THE NOISE WHICH HAD DISTURBED HIS PEACEFUL WAY.

TARZAN LAUGHED ALOUD AND
CAME CLOSER ABOVE THE HEAD OF THE
PACHYDERM. "TANTOR! TANTOR!"
HE CRIED. "BARA, THE DEER, IS
LESS FEARFUL THAN YOU -- YOU,
TANTOR, THE ELEPHANT,
GREATEST OF THE JUNGLE
FOLK, WHO TREMBLES
WITH FEAR AT THE
SOUND OF A
BROKEN TWIG."

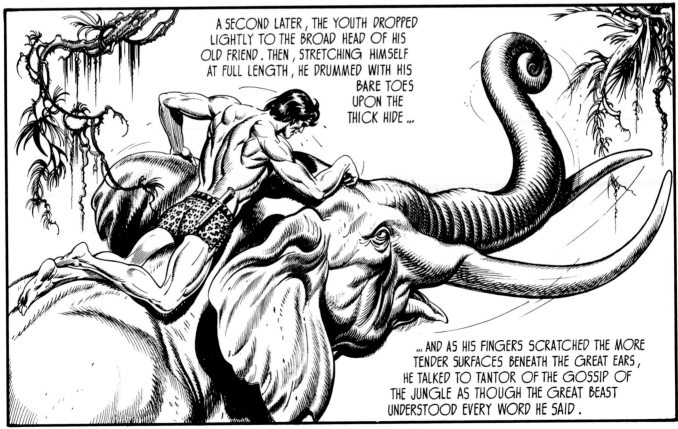

A SECOND LATER, THE YOUTH DROPPED
LIGHTLY TO THE BROAD HEAD OF HIS
OLD FRIEND. THEN, STRETCHING HIMSELF
AT FULL LENGTH, HE DRUMMED WITH HIS
BARE TOES
UPON THE
THICK HIDE ...

... AND AS HIS FINGERS SCRATCHED THE MORE
TENDER SURFACES BENEATH THE GREAT EARS,
HE TALKED TO TANTOR OF THE GOSSIP OF
THE JUNGLE AS THOUGH THE GREAT BEAST
UNDERSTOOD EVERY WORD HE SAID.

MUCH THERE WAS WHICH TARZAN COULD MAKE
TANTOR UNDERSTAND, AND THOUGH THE SMALL
TALK OF THE WILD WAS BEYOND THE GREAT,
GRAY DREADNOUGHT OF THE JUNGLE ...

...HE STOOD WITH BLINKING
EYES AND GENTLY SWAYING TRUNK
AS THOUGH DRINKING IN EVERY WORD
OF IT WITH KEENEST APPRECIATION.

FOR AN HOUR
TARZAN SPRAWLED
THERE UPON
TANTOR'S
BACK.

TIME HAD NO
MEANING FOR
EITHER OF THEM.

IT WAS RESTFUL AND SATISFYING TO
SPRAWL UPON HIS ROUGH PATE AND
POUR ONE'S VAGUE HOPES AND
ASPIRATIONS INTO THE GREAT EARS
WHICH FLAPPED PONDEROUSLY TO
AND FRO IN APPARENT UNDER-
STANDING. OF ALL THE
JUNGLE FOLK, TANTOR
COMMANDED TARZAN'S
GREATEST LOVE SINCE
KALA HAD
BEEN
TAKEN
FROM
HIM.

IT WAS THE CALL OF THE STOMACH---THE MOST COMPELLING AND INSISTENT CALL WHICH THE JUNGLE KNOWS...

...THAT TOOK TARZAN FINALLY BACK TO THE TREES AND OFF IN SEARCH OF FOOD, WHILE TANTOR ...

...CONTINUED HIS INTERRUPTED JOURNEY IN THE OPPOSITE DIRECTION .

...HIS ACTIVE MIND BUSIED ITSELF NOT ALONE WITH HIS HUNTING , BUT WITH MANY OTHER SUBJECTS .

AND AS HE ROAMED THE JUNGLE ...

HE HAD A HABIT OF RECALLING THE EVENTS OF THE PRE- CEDING DAYS .

HE LIVED OVER HIS VISIT WITH TANTOR---

--HE COGITATED UPON THE DIGGING BLACKS AND THE STRANGE, COVERED PIT THEY HAD LEFT BEHIND THEM .

AND AS HE PUZZLED OVER THE COVERED PIT, THERE LOOMED SUDDENLY BEFORE HIS MENTAL VISION A HUGE, GRAY-BLACK BULK WHICH LUMBERED PONDEROUSLY ALONG A JUNGLE TRAIL.

HOGARTH=

INSTANTLY TARZAN TENSED.

DECISION AND ACTION USUALLY OCCURRED SIMULTANEOUSLY IN THE LIFE OF THE APE-MAN, AND NOW HE WAS AWAY THROUGH THE LEAFY BRANCHES ERE THE REALIZATION OF THE PIT'S PURPOSE HAD SCARCE FORMED IN HIS MIND.

SWINGING FROM SWAYING LIMB TO SWAYING LIMB, HE RACED THROUGH THE MIDDLE TERRACES WHERE THE TREES GREW CLOSE TOGETHER.

HOGARTH

AGAIN HE DROPPED TO THE GROUND AND SPED, SILENTLY AND LIGHT OF FOOT, OVER THE CARPET OF DECAYING VEGETATION...

...ONLY TO LEAP AGAIN INTO THE TREES WHERE THE TANGLED UNDER-GROWTH PRECLUDED RAPID ADVANCE UPON THE SURFACE.

IN HIS ANXIETY, HE CAST DISCRETION TO THE WINDS. THE CAUTION OF THE BEAST WAS LOST IN THE LOYALTY OF THE MAN, AND SO IT CAME THAT HE ENTERED A LARGE CLEARING, DENUDED OF TREES, WITHOUT A THOUGHT OF WHAT MIGHT LIE THERE OR UPON THE FARTHER EDGE TO DISPUTE THE WAY WITH HIM.
HE WAS HALF WAY ACROSS WHEN, DIRECTLY IN HIS PATH AND BUT A FEW YARDS AWAY, THERE ROSE FROM A CLUMP OF TALL GRASSES A RUSH OF CHATTERING BIRDS.

INSTANTLY TARZAN TURNED ASIDE, FOR HE KNEW WELL ENOUGH WHAT MANNER OF CREATURE THE PRESENCE OF THESE LITTLE SENTINELS PROCLAIMED. SIMULTANEOUSLY, THE SNORTS OF THE ANGRY BEAST SENT THEM SCURRYING AFFRIGHTEDLY TO THE UPPER TERRACES.

BUTO, THE RHINOCEROS, SCRAMBLED TO HIS SHORT LEGS, SHOOK HIS GREAT BULK, AND STARTED A FURIOUS CHARGE.

DIRECTLY IN THE PATH OF THE CHARGE STOOD TARZAN.

AND NOW BUTO WAS UPON HIM, THE MASSIVE HEAD WITH ITS LONG, HEAVY HORN INCLINED FOR ITS FRIGHTFUL WORK.

BUT AS BUTO STRUCK UPWARD, HIS HORN RAKED ONLY THIN AIR, FOR THE APE-MAN HAD SWUNG LIGHTLY ALOFT WITH A CATLIKE LEAP ...

...THAT CARRIED HIM ABOVE THE THREATENING HORN ...

...TO THE BROAD BACK OF THE RHINOCEROS

ANOTHER SPRING AND HE WAS ON THE GROUND...

...BEHIND THE BRUTE AND RACING LIKE A DEER FOR THE TREES.

SOME DISTANCE AHEAD OF HIM, TANTOR MOVED STEADILY ALONG THE WELL-WORN ELEPHANT TRAIL ...

...AND AHEAD OF TANTOR WARRIOR SCOUTS LISTENED INTENTLY FOR HIS COMING.

TO HIS RIGHT AND LEFT IN OTHER PARTS OF THE JUNGLE, OTHER WARRIORS WERE WATCHING. SILENTLY THEY WAITED ...

...AND PRESENTLY WERE REWARDED BY THE SIGHT OF A MIGHTY TUSKER.

NO SOONER HAD HE PASSED THEIR POSITIONS THAN THE WARRIORS CLAMBERED FROM THEIR PERCHES. NO LONGER WERE THEY SILENT, BUT INSTEAD CLAPPED THEIR HANDS AND SHOUTED AS THEY REACHED THE GROUND.

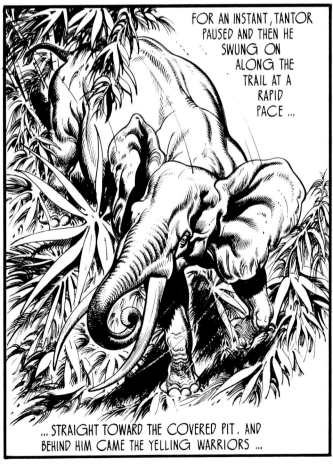

FOR AN INSTANT, TANTOR PAUSED AND THEN HE SWUNG ON ALONG THE TRAIL AT A RAPID PACE ...

... STRAIGHT TOWARD THE COVERED PIT. AND BEHIND HIM CAME THE YELLING WARRIORS ...

... PROVOKING HIM IN A HEAD-LONG FLIGHT WHICH WOULD NOT PERMIT A CAREFUL TESTING OF THE TRAIL. TANTOR, WHO COULD HAVE SCATTERED HIS ADVERSARIES WITH A SINGLE CHARGE, FLED LIKE A FRIGHTENED DEER -- FLED TOWARD A HIDEOUS, TORTURING DEATH.

AND BEHIND THEM ALL CAME TARZAN OF THE APES ...

...RACING THROUGH THE FOREST WITH THE SPEED AND AGILITY OF A SQUIRREL ...

...FOR HE HAD HEARD THE SHOUTS OF THE WARRIORS AND HAD INTERPRETED THEM CORRECTLY .

NOW THE GIANT PACHYDERM WAS BUT YARDS FROM THE HIDDEN DEATH LURKING IN HIS PATH , AND THE BLACKS , CERTAIN OF SUCCESS , WERE SCREAMING AND DANCING IN HIS WAKE , CELE- BRATING IN ADVANCE THE ACQUISITION OF THE SPLENDID IVORY CARRIED BY THEIR PREY .

HOGARTH

A FEW MORE STEPS WOULD PRECIPITATE TANTOR UPON THE SHARPENED STAKES; TARZAN FAIRLY FLEW THROUGH THE TREES UNTIL HE HAD COME ABREAST OF THE FLEEING ANIMAL AND THEN HAD PASSED HIM. AT THE PIT'S VERGE, THE APE-MAN DROPPED TO THE GROUND IN THE CENTER OF THE TRAIL. TANTOR WAS ALMOST UPON HIM BEFORE HIS WEAK EYES PERMITTED HIM TO RECOGNIZE HIS OLD FRIEND. "STOP!" CRIED TARZAN, AND THE GREAT BEAST HALTED TO THE UPRAISED HAND.

TARZAN TURNED AND KICKED ASIDE
SOME OF THE BRUSH WHICH HID THE PIT.
INSTANTLY TANTOR SAW AND UNDERSTOOD.

"FIGHT!" GROWLED TARZAN. "THEY ARE COMING BEHIND YOU."

BUT TANTOR WAS PANIC-STRICKEN BY TERROR. BEFORE HIM
YAWNED THE PIT; TO THE RIGHT AND LEFT LAY THE PRIMITIVE JUNGLE.
WITH A SQUEAL, THE GREAT BEAST TURNED SUDDENLY AT RIGHT
ANGLES AND BURST THROUGH THE SOLID WALL OF VEGETATION
THAT WOULD HAVE STOPPED ANY BUT HIM.

TARZAN,
STANDING AT
THE EDGE OF
THE PIT,
SUDDENLY
FELT THE
EARTH
GIVE WAY,
BACKWARD
AND
DOWNWARD...

...HE WENT
TOWARD
THE
SHARPENED
STAKES.

WHEN, A MOMENT LATER, THE BLACKS CAME UP
AND PEERED INTO THE PIT, THEIR EYES WENT WIDE
IN ASTONISHMENT; INSTEAD OF AN ELEPHANT, AT
THE BOTTOM LAY THE STILL FIGURE
OF A WHITE GIANT.

SEVERAL WARRIORS LEAPED INTO THE PIT AND LIFTED
TARZAN OUT. IN FALLING, HIS HEAD HAD STRUCK
A STAKE, RENDERING HIM UNCONSCIOUS.
SEEING THIS,
THEY BROUGHT
HIM UP ...

... AND BOUND HIS ARMS. THE APE-MAN'S
EYE-LIDS QUIVERED AND OPENED. THEY
SET HIM ON HIS FEET AND FORCED HIM
FORWARD WITH SPEARS, YET WITH EVERY
MANIFESTATION OF THE SUPERSTITIOUS
AWE IN WHICH THEY HELD HIM.

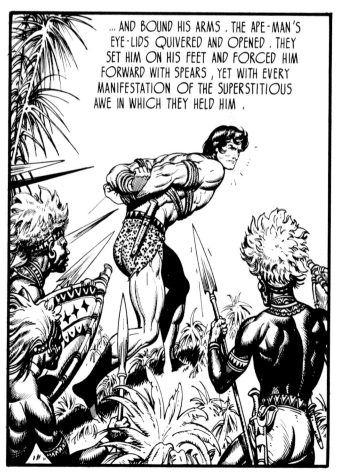

AS THEY APPROACHED THEIR VILLAGE, THE WARRIORS SHOUTED ALOUD THEIR VICTORIOUS CRIES, SO THAT BY THE TIME THEY REACHED THE GATE, A GREAT THRONG OF MEN, WOMEN, AND CHILDREN WERE GATHERED TO GREET THEM AND HEAR OF THEIR GREAT ADVENTURE.

AS THE EYES OF THE VILLAGERS FELL UPON THE PRISONER, THEY WENT WILD WITH ASTONISHMENT AND INCREDULITY. FOR MONTHS THEY HAD LIVED IN TERROR OF A WEIRD, WHITE DEMON WHOM BUT FEW HAD EVER GLIMPSED AND LIVED TO DESCRIBE.

BUT NOW HE WAS IN THEIR POWER!
NO LONGER COULD HE
TERRORIZE THEM.

SLOWLY THE REALIZATION OF THIS DAWNED UPON THEM.
ONE VILLAGER, THEN ANOTHER AND ANOTHER,
CAME CLOSE TO HURL INVECTIVE ...

...UNTIL TARZAN WAS SURROUNDED BY A
YELLING FORCE OF MBONGA'S TRIBE.

AND THEN MBONGA,
THE CHIEF, CAME, ...

...LAYING HIS SPEAR HEAVILY ACROSS THE
SHOULDERS OF HIS PEOPLE, AND DROVE
THEM FROM THEIR PREY. "WE WILL SAVE
HIM UNTIL NIGHT," HE SAID.

FAR OUT IN THE JUNGLE, TANTOR, HIS FIRST PANIC OF
FEAR ALLAYED, STOOD WITH UPRAISED EARS AND UNDULATING TRUNK. THE SCREAMS
OF THE INFURIATED VILLAGERS CAME FAINTLY TO HIS SENSITIVE EARS.

HE WHEELED, AS THOUGH IN TERROR,
CONTEMPLATING FLIGHT ...

...BUT SOMETHING STAYED
HIM, AND AGAIN HE TURNED,
RAISED HIS TRUNK, AND GAVE
VOICE TO A SHRILL CRY.

THEN HE STOOD
LISTENING ...

IN THE DISTANT VILLAGE, WHERE MBONGA HAD RESTORED QUIET AND ORDER, THE VOICE OF TANTOR WAS SCARCELY AUDIBLE TO THE BLACKS ...

...BUT TO THE KEEN EARS OF TARZAN OF THE APES IT BORE ITS MESSAGE. HE HALTED AS HE HEARD THE NOTES OF TANTOR'S CALL, AND RAISING HIS HEAD ...

... GAVE VENT TO A TERRIFYING SCREAM THAT CAUSED HIS GUARDS TO LEAP BACK EVEN THOUGH THE PRISONER'S ARMS WERE SECURELY BOUND.

WITH RAISED SPEARS THEY ENCIRCLED HIM AS, FOR A MOMENT LONGER, HE STOOD LISTENING.

FAINTLY FROM THE DISTANCE CAME ANOTHER, AN ANSWERING CRY, AND TARZAN OF THE APES, SATISFIED, TURNED AND QUIETLY PURSUED HIS CAPTORS TO THE HUT WHERE HE WAS TO BE IMPRISONED.

THE AFTERNOON WORE ON. FROM THE SURROUNDING VILLAGE, THE
APE-MAN HEARD THE BUSTLE OF PREPARATION FOR THE FEAST.

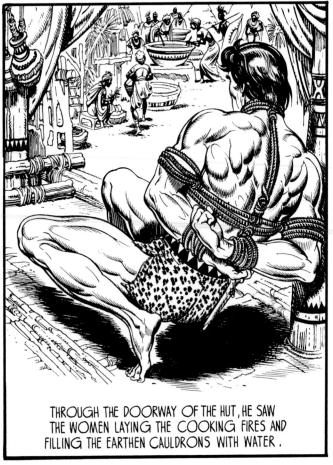

THROUGH THE DOORWAY OF THE HUT, HE SAW
THE WOMEN LAYING THE COOKING FIRES AND
FILLING THE EARTHEN CAULDRONS WITH WATER.

BUT ABOVE IT ALL, HIS
EARS WERE BENT ACROSS
THE JUNGLE IN EAGER LISTENING
FOR THE COMING OF TANTOR.

EVEN TARZAN BUT HALF BELIEVED THAT TANTOR WOULD COME.

ALL AFTERNOON HE HAD BEEN WORKING WITH THE BONDS THAT HELD HIS WRISTS. HE KNEW TANTOR EVEN BETTER THAN TANTOR KNEW HIMSELF. HE KNEW THE TIMID HEART WHICH LAY IN THE GIANT BODY. HE KNEW THE PANIC OF TERROR WHICH THE GOMANGANI INSPIRED IN HIM, AND AS NIGHT DREW ON, HOPE DIED IN TARZAN'S BREAST, AND IN THE STOIC CALM OF THE WILD BEAST WHICH HE WAS, HE RESIGNED HIMSELF TO MEET THE FATE WHICH AWAITED HIM.

AT LAST THEY CAME --- MBONGA'S BEFEATHERED WARRIORS --- PUSHING HIM INTO THE OPEN, WHERE HE WAS GREETED BY WILD SHOUTS FROM THE THRONG.

IN THE FLICKERING
TORCHLIGHT OF THE
ALTAR, HE WAS LED TO THE
STAKE THAT WOULD SECURE
HIM FOR THE DANCE OF DEATH.
TARZAN TENSED HIS MUSCLES.
IF HE COULD BUT FREE
HIS ARMS ...

MBONGA RAISED HIS SPEAR AND A HUSH FELL OVER
THE CROWD. IN THAT INSTANT, TARZAN FLEXED WITH
A POWERFUL SURGE OF HIS MIGHTY THEWS AND
WITH A SINGLE WRENCH THE THONGS PARTED
WHICH SECURED HIS HANDS.

LIKE THOUGHT, FOR QUICKNESS, HE LEAPED AMONG THE WARRIORS NEAREST HIM. A BLOW SENT ONE TO EARTH, AS, GROWLING AND SNARLING, THE BEAST-MAN SURGED OUTWARD.

A HALF HUNDRED BLACK MEN HAD LEAPED UPON HIM. STRIKING AND CLAWING AND SNAPPING, THE APE-MAN FOUGHT -- FOUGHT AS HIS FOSTER PEOPLE HAD TAUGHT HIM TO FIGHT -- FOUGHT LIKE A WILD BEAST CORNERED.

HOGARTH=

BUT NOT EVEN TARZAN OF THE APES
COULD HOPE SUCCESSFULLY TO COPE
WITH SUCH A SUPERIOR FORCE. SLOWLY
THEY WERE OVERPOWERING HIM.

OVERPOWER HIM THEY MIGHT, BUT COULD THEY KEEP HIM SUFFICIENTLY SUBDUED WHILE THEY BOUND HIM?
A HALF HOUR OF FURIOUS AND CONVULSIVE STRUGGLE CONVINCED THEM THEY COULD NOT.

IN THE DESPERATE ENDEAVOR, MBONGA CALLED TO A WARRIOR TO CLOSE IN AND SPEAR THE VICTIM.

THE MAN MOVED UP, SPEAR POISED, READY FOR A FATAL THRUST.

HE AIMED THE WEAPON; AND THEN FROM THE JUNGLE BEYOND THE PALISADE CAME A THUNDEROUS CRASHING.

IN THE GLARE OF THE FIRES, THE WARRIORS SAW A HUGE BULK TOPPING THE BARRIER. THEY SAW THE PALISADE BELLY AND SWAY INWARD.

THEY SAW IT BURST AS THOUGH BUILT OF STRAWS ...

... AND AN INSTANT LATER, TANTOR, THE ELEPHANT, THUNDERED DOWN UPON THEM.

WARRIORS FLED SCREAMING IN TERROR BEFORE THE APPROACH OF THE GIANT TUSKER. TANTOR CHARGED INTO THE MELEE, TRUMPETING FURIOUSLY. HE FOUND TARZAN, BLOODY, BUT STILL BATTLING. ONE AFTER ANOTHER, TANTOR WRENCHED THE BLACKS FROM THE BODY OF THE APE-MAN, THROWING THEM RIGHT AND LEFT. ONE AFTER ANOTHER, THE SINUOUS TRUNK ENCIRCLED SEVERAL WARRIORS AND FLUNG THEM FAR AFTER THE FLEEING CROWD.

AT A DISTANCE, MBONGA RALLIED HIS
WARRIORS. HIS GREEDY EYES HAD NOTED THE
GREAT IVORY TUSKS OF THE BULL, AND AS THE FIRST
PANIC OF TERROR BROKE, HE URGED HIS
MEN FORWARD TO ATTACK WITH THEIR
HEAVY ELEPHANT SPEARS.

BUT AS THEY CAME,
TANTOR SWUNG
TARZAN ALOFT.

THE GREAT BEAST WHEELED, AND WITH HIS PRECIOUS BURDEN HELD HIGH, PLUNGED THROUGH THE GREAT RENT HE HAD MADE IN THE PALISADE ...

...AND LUMBERED OFF INTO THE JUNGLE, SEEKING SAFETY IN THE MISTY SHADOWS OF THE NIGHT.

HOGARTH=

AND SO IT WAS THAT TANTOR,
THE ELEPHANT, DISCHARGED AN
OBLIGATION TO TARZAN OF THE
APES, CEMENTING EVER MORE CLOSELY THE FRIENDSHIP THAT HAD EXISTED BETWEEN THEM SINCE TARZAN, AS A
LITTLE, BROWN BOY, RODE UPON TANTOR'S HUGE BACK THROUGH THE MOONLIT JUNGLE BENEATH THE EQUATORIAL STARS.

BOOK THREE

The God of Tarzan

AMONG THE BOOKS OF HIS DEAD FATHER IN THE LITTLE CABIN BY THE LAND-LOCKED HARBOR, TARZAN OF THE APES FOUND MANY THINGS TO PUZZLE HIS YOUNG HEAD. BY MUCH LABOR AND THROUGH THE MEDIUM OF INFINITE PATIENCE...

...HE HAD, WITHOUT ASSISTANCE, DISCOVERED THE PURPOSE OF THE LITTLE BUGS WHICH RAN RIOT ON THE PRINTED PAGES.

HE HAD LEARNED THAT, IN THE MANY COMBINATIONS, THEY SPOKE IN A SILENT LANGUAGE, SPOKE OF WONDERFUL THINGS WHICH A LITTLE APE-BOY COULD NOT FULLY UNDERSTAND, AROUSING HIS CURIOSITY AND FILLING HIS SOUL WITH A MIGHTY LONGING FOR FURTHER KNOWLEDGE.

A DICTIONARY HAD PROVEN ITSELF A WONDERFUL STOREHOUSE OF INFORMATION, WHEN, AFTER SEVERAL YEARS OF TIRELESS ENDEAVOR, HE HAD SOLVED THE MYSTERY OF ITS PURPOSE AND THE MANNER OF ITS USE. HE HAD LEARNED TO MAKE A SPECIES OF GAME OUT OF IT, FOLLOWING UP THE SPOOR OF EACH NEW THOUGHT THROUGH THE MAZES OF THE MANY DEFINITIONS WHICH EACH NEW WORD REQUIRED HIM TO CONSULT. IT WAS LIKE FOLLOWING A QUARRY THROUGH THE JUNGLE -- IT WAS HUNTING, AND TARZAN OF THE APES WAS AN INDEFATIGABLE HUNTSMAN.

THERE WERE, OF COURSE, CERTAIN WORDS WHICH AROUSED HIS CURIOSITY TO A GREATER EXTENT THAN OTHERS, WORDS WHICH, FOR ONE REASON OR ANOTHER, EXCITED HIS IMAGINATION. THERE WAS ONE, FOR EXAMPLE, THE MEANING OF WHICH WAS RATHER DIFFICULT TO GRASP. IT WAS THE WORD *GOD*.

TARZAN FIRST HAD BEEN ATTRACTED TO IT BY THE FACT THAT IT WAS VERY SHORT AND THAT IT COMMENCED WITH A LARGER G-BUG THAN THOSE ABOUT IT -- A MALE G-BUG IT WAS TO TARZAN, THE LOWER-CASE LETTERS BEING FEMALES. ANOTHER FACT WHICH ATTRACTED HIM TO THIS WORD WAS THE NUMBER OF HE-BUGS WHICH FIGURED IN ITS DEFINITION -- *SUPREME DEITY, CREATOR OR UPHOLDER OF THE UNIVERSE.*

THIS MUST BE A VERY IMPORTANT WORD INDEED. HE WOULD HAVE TO LOOK INTO IT, AND HE DID, THOUGH IT STILL BAFFLED HIM AFTER MANY MONTHS OF THOUGHT AND STUDY.

ONCE HE THOUGHT HE HAD GRASPED IT -- THAT GOD WAS A MIGHTY CHIEFTAIN, KING OF ALL THE MANGANI,

HE WAS NOT QUITE SURE, HOWEVER, SINCE THAT WOULD MEAN THAT GOD WAS MIGHTIER THAN TARZAN -- A POINT WHICH TARZAN OF THE APES, WHO ACKNOWLEDGED NO EQUAL IN THE JUNGLE, WAS LOATH TO CONCEDE.

FINALLY HE BEGAN TO WONDER IF GOD WERE NOT OF A DIFFERENT FORM THAN HE, AND AT LAST HE DETERMINED TO SET OUT IN SEARCH OF HIM.

HE COMMENCED BY QUESTIONING MUMGA, WHO WAS VERY OLD ...

...AND HAD SEEN MANY STRANGE THINGS IN HER LONG LIFE;

BUT MUMGA HAD A FACULTY FOR RECALLING THE TRIVIAL.

THAT TIME WHEN GUNTO MISTOOK A STING-BUG FOR AN EDIBLE BEETLE HAD MADE MORE IMPRESSION UPON MUMGA THAN ALL THE MANIFESTATIONS OF GOD WHICH SHE HAD WITNESSED, BUT WHICH, OF COURSE, SHE HAD NOT UNDERSTOOD.

NUMGO, OVERHEARING TARZAN'S QUESTIONS, ADVANCED THE THEORY ...

...THAT THE POWER WHICH MADE THE LIGHTNING AND THE RAIN AND THE THUNDER CAME FROM GORO, THE MOON.

HE KNEW THIS, HE SAID, BECAUSE THE DUM-DUM ALWAYS WAS DANCED IN THE LIGHT OF GORO.

THAT NIGHT, THE MOON WAS FULL, A GLORIOUS, EQUATORIAL MOON. IN ORDER TO INVESTIGATE IT MORE CLOSELY, THE APE-MAN CLAMBERED TO THE LOFTIEST PINNACLE OF THE TALLEST JUNGLE GIANT.

TO HIS SURPRISE, HE FOUND THAT GORO WAS AS FAR AWAY AS WHEN HE VIEWED HIM FROM THE GROUND.

HE THOUGHT GORO WAS ATTEMPTING TO ELUDE HIM. "COME, GORO!" HE CRIED, "TARZAN OF THE APES WILL NOT HARM YOU!"

BUT STILL THE MOON HELD ALOOF. "TELL ME," HE CONTINUED, "IF YOU BE THE GREAT KING WHO SENDS ARA, THE LIGHTNING; WHO MAKES THE GREAT NOISE AND THE MIGHTY WINDS, AND SENDS THE WATERS DOWN UPON THE JUNGLE PEOPLE,"

"TELL ME, GORO-- ARE YOU GOD?"

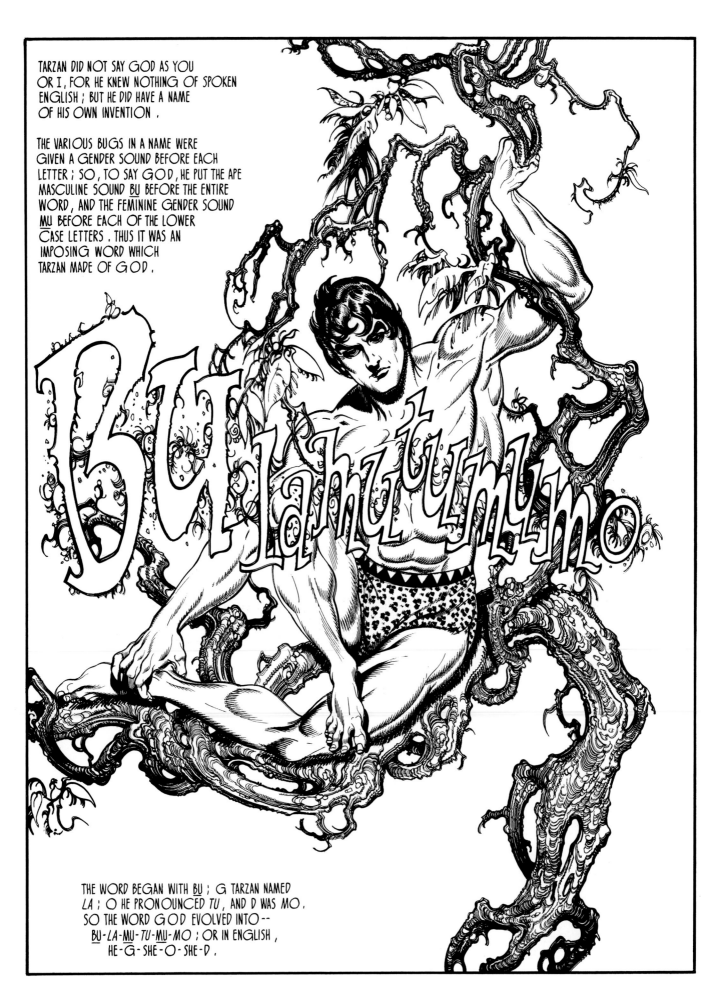

TARZAN DID NOT SAY GOD AS YOU
OR I, FOR HE KNEW NOTHING OF SPOKEN
ENGLISH ; BUT HE DID HAVE A NAME
OF HIS OWN INVENTION .

THE VARIOUS BUGS IN A NAME WERE
GIVEN A GENDER SOUND BEFORE EACH
LETTER ; SO, TO SAY GOD, HE PUT THE APE
MASCULINE SOUND BU BEFORE THE ENTIRE
WORD, AND THE FEMININE GENDER SOUND
MU BEFORE EACH OF THE LOWER
CASE LETTERS . THUS IT WAS AN
IMPOSING WORD WHICH
TARZAN MADE OF GOD .

THE WORD BEGAN WITH BU ; G TARZAN NAMED
LA ; O HE PRONOUNCED TU, AND D WAS MO.
SO THE WORD GOD EVOLVED INTO --
BU-LA-MU-TU-MU-MO ; OR IN ENGLISH ,
HE-G-SHE-O-SHE-D .

AND SO TARZAN HARANGUED THE MOON, AND WHEN GORO DID NOT REPLY, TARZAN OF THE APES WAXED WROTH. HE SWELLED HIS GIANT CHEST AND BARED HIS FIGHTING FANGS AND HURLED INTO THE TEETH OF THE DEAD SATELLITE THE CHALLENGE OF THE BULL APE. "YOU ARE NOT BULAMUTUMUMO," HE CRIED. "YOU ARE NOT KING OF THE JUNGLE FOLK."

"YOU ARE NOT SO GREAT AS TARZAN, MIGHTY FIGHTER, MIGHTY HUNTER. IF THERE BE A BULAMUTUMUMO, TARZAN CAN KILL HIM, COME DOWN, GORO, AND FIGHT WITH TARZAN. I AM TARZAN, THE KILLER."

BUT GORO MADE NO
ANSWER; AND WHEN A CLOUD
OBSCURED ITS FACE, TARZAN
THOUGHT GORO WAS
INDEED AFRAID.

SO HE CAME DOWN AND TOLD NUMGO HE HAD FRIGHT-
ENED GORO OUT OF THE SKY. "NOW WHERE SHALL I
FIND GOD?" HE INSISTED. "I AM GOD," SAID NUMGO.
"NOW SLEEP AND DISTURB ME NO MORE."

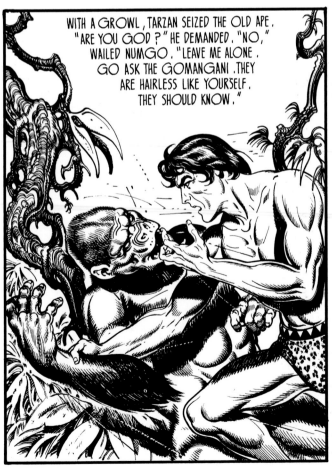

WITH A GROWL, TARZAN SEIZED THE OLD APE.
"ARE YOU GOD?" HE DEMANDED. "NO,"
WAILED NUMGO. "LEAVE ME ALONE.
GO ASK THE GOMANGANI. THEY
ARE HAIRLESS LIKE YOURSELF.
THEY SHOULD KNOW."

SO TARZAN SPED TOWARD THE VILLAGE OF MBONGA. HE
WISHED TO SPEAK TO THE CREATOR OF THE UNIVERSE, SO
HE HOPED GOD WOULD NOT PROVE BELLIGERENT. BUT HE
WAS READY WITH ROPE, SPEAR, AND POISONED ARROWS
IF GOD WISHED TO FIGHT.

IT WAS DARK WHEN TARZAN CAME TO
THE GREAT TREE ABOVE MBONGA'S VILLAGE.
BELOW MOVED A GROTESQUE FIGURE THAT WENT
ON THE LEGS OF A MAN, YET HAD THE HEAD OF A
BUFFALO. TARZAN WAS ELECTRIFIED. COULD
IT BE THAT HE LOOKED UPON GOD?

THE VILLAGERS FELL BACK IN TERROR...

...AS THE APPARITION LEAPED ABOUT.
WATCHING, TARZAN WAS CON-
VINCED HIS EYES WERE
UPON GOD.

A LION ROARED SUDDENLY OUTSIDE THE PALISADE. THE
BLACKS FELL SILENT, AND THE WITCH-DOCTOR PAUSED,
MOMENTARILY RIGID. IT WAS THIS MOMENT THAT TARZAN
CHOSE TO DROP LIGHTLY INTO THE VILLAGE.

209

MUSCLED LIKE NUMA, THE LION, TARZAN STRODE STRAIGHT TO THE HIDEOUS FIGURE. EVERY EYE WAS UPON HIM, YET NO ONE MOVED. "ARE YOU GOD?" ASKED TARZAN.

THE WITCH-DOCTOR, UNDERSTANDING NONE OF TARZAN'S WORDS, LEAPED HIGH IN THE AIR, WHIRLED, AND ALIGHTED WITH OUTSPREAD ARMS UTTERING A BLOOD-CURDLING CRY.

TARZAN DID NOT PAUSE. HE HAD SET OUT TO APPROACH AND EXAMINE GOD, AND NOTHING ON EARTH MIGHT NOW STAY HIS QUEST.

SEEING THAT HIS ANTICS HAD NO POTENCY WITH THE VISITOR, THE WITCH-DOCTOR TRIED SOME NEW MEDICINE, MEANWHILE BACKING CAUTIOUSLY AWAY FROM TARZAN, FOR THE APE-MAN WAS STEADILY CLOSING THE GAP WHICH SEPARATED THEM.

"STOP!" HE CRIED, AND DREW AN IMAGINARY LINE. "BEYOND THIS LINE YOU CANNOT PASS OR YOU WILL DIE!"

TARZAN OF THE APES CROSSED THE MAGICAL LINE AND STILL LIVED,

THE WITCH-DOCTOR TURNED AND FLED.

"COME BACK, GOD!" TARZAN CRIED, "I WILL NOT HARM YOU."

THE APE-MAN BORE DOWN ON HIM WITH THE SPEED OF BARA, THE DEER, OVERHAULED HIM AT THE ENTRANCE TO HIS HUT ...

... AND RIPPED THE DISGUISE FROM HIM. IT WAS A NAKED, TERROR-STRICKEN BLACK MAN THAT TARZAN SAW. SO THIS WAS WHAT HE THOUGHT WAS GOD!

TARZAN SEIZED THE CRINGING FIGURE. "IF YOU ARE GOD," HE CRIED, "THEN TARZAN IS GREATER THAN GOD."

"WITH HIS OWN HANDS HE HAS SLAIN NUMA, THE LION. SEE!" HE GAVE A SUDDEN WRENCH AND THE FELLOW SHRIEKED AND SLUMPED TO EARTH IN A SWOON ...

... AND NOW RANG THROUGH THE AIR ...

... THE SCREAM OF VICTORY OF THE BULL APE.

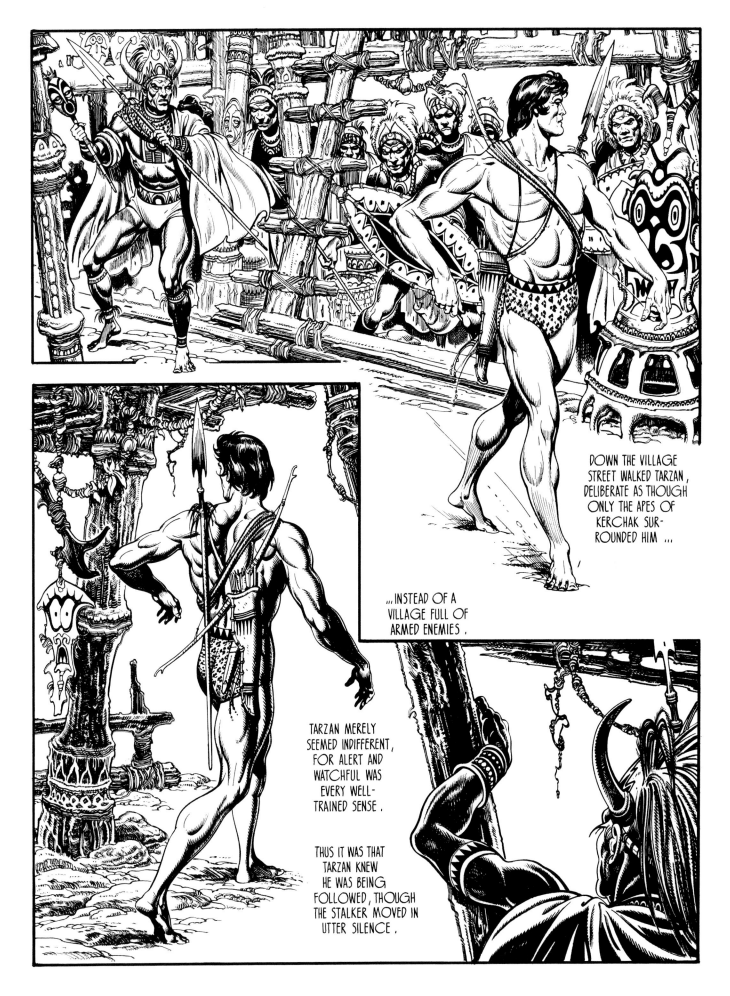

DOWN THE VILLAGE STREET WALKED TARZAN, DELIBERATE AS THOUGH ONLY THE APES OF KERCHAK SURROUNDED HIM ...

...INSTEAD OF A VILLAGE FULL OF ARMED ENEMIES.

TARZAN MERELY SEEMED INDIFFERENT, FOR ALERT AND WATCHFUL WAS EVERY WELL-TRAINED SENSE.

THUS IT WAS THAT TARZAN KNEW HE WAS BEING FOLLOWED, THOUGH THE STALKER MOVED IN UTTER SILENCE.

WHEN MBONGA CAME, THEREFORE, WITHIN SPEAR RANGE OF THE APE-MAN, THE LATTER SUDDENLY WHEELED UPON HIM, SO SUDDENLY THAT THE POISED SPEAR WAS SHOT A FRACTION OF A SECOND BEFORE MBONGA HAD INTENDED, TARZAN DODGED TO LET IT PASS OVER HIS HEAD...

... THEN HE SPRANG TOWARD THE CHIEF WITH THE SPEED OF A CHARGING LION.

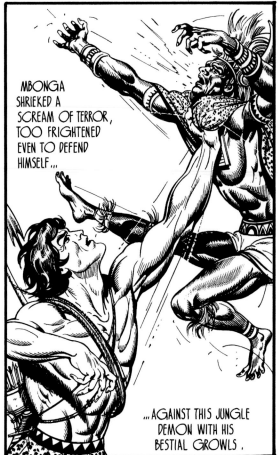

MBONGA SHRIEKED A SCREAM OF TERROR, TOO FRIGHTENED EVEN TO DEFEND HIMSELF...

... AGAINST THIS JUNGLE DEMON WITH HIS BESTIAL GROWLS.

TARZAN LOWERED THE CHIEF AND LOOKED HIM
IN THE FACE. HE DREW HIS LONG, KEEN KNIFE AND RAISED IT CLOSE TO MBONGA'S NECK.
THE OLD WARRIOR BROKE AND PLEADED FOR HIS LIFE IN A TONGUE WHICH TARZAN COULD NOT UNDERSTAND.

FOR THE FIRST TIME, THE APE-MAN HAD A CLOSE VIEW
OF THE CHIEF. HE SAW A VERY OLD MAN WITH
SCRAWNY NECK AND WRINKLED FACE.

NEVER BEFORE HAD TARZAN SEEN SUCH TERROR IN THE EYES
OF ANY ANIMAL, OR SUCH A PITEOUS APPEAL FOR MERCY
UPON THE FACE OF ANY CREATURE.

SOMETHING STAYED THE
APE-MAN'S HAND FOR
AN INSTANT.

HE WONDERED WHY IT WAS THAT HE HESITATED TO
MAKE THE KILL. NEVER BEFORE HAD HE THUS DELAYED ...

215

THE OLD MAN SEEMED TO WITHER BENEATH HIS EYES. SO WEAK AND HELPLESS HE APPEARED THAT THE APE-MAN WAS FILLED WITH A GREAT CONTEMPT; BUT ANOTHER SENSATION CLAIMED HIM -- SOMETHING NEW TO TARZAN OF THE APES IN RELATION TO AN ENEMY. IT WAS PITY -- PITY FOR A POOR, FRIGHTENED OLD MAN.

TARZAN ROSE AND TURNED AWAY, LEAVING MBONGA UNHARMED. WITH HEAD HELD HIGH, THE APE-MAN WALKED THROUGH THE VILLAGE...

... SWUNG HIMSELF INTO THE TREE WHICH OVERHUNG THE PALISADE, AND DISAPPEARED FROM THE SIGHT OF THE VILLAGERS.

ALL THE WAY BACK TO THE
STAMPING GROUND OF THE
APES, TARZAN SOUGHT FOR AN
EXPLANATION OF THE STRANGE POWER WHICH
HAD STAYED HIS HAND AND PREVENTED HIM FROM SLAYING
MBONGA. IT WAS AS THOUGH SOMEONE GREATER THAN HE HAD
COMMANDED HIM TO SPARE THE LIFE OF THE OLD MAN. TARZAN COULD NOT UNDERSTAND, FOR HE COULD CONCEIVE OF NOTHING,
OR NO ONE, WITH THE AUTHORITY TO DICTATE TO HIM WHAT HE SHOULD DO OR REFRAIN FROM DOING.

IT WAS LATE
WHEN TARZAN
SOUGHT A
SWAYING
COUCH
AMONG THE
TREES BENEATH
WHICH SLEPT
THE APES OF
KERCHAK ...

...AND HE WAS STILL ABSORBED IN THE SOLUTION OF HIS STRANGE PROBLEM WHEN HE FELL ASLEEP.

THE SUN WAS WELL UP IN THE HEAVENS
WHEN HE AWOKE. THE APES WERE ASTIR
IN SEARCH OF FOOD. TARZAN WATCHED
THEM LAZILY FROM ABOVE. AN ORCHID
DANGLING CLOSE BESIDE HIS HEAD OPENED
SLOWLY, UNFOLDING ITS DELICATE PETALS TO
THE WARMTH AND LIGHT OF THE SUN. A THOUSAND
TIMES HAD TARZAN OF THE APES WITNESSED THE
BEAUTEOUS MIRACLE ; BUT NOW IT AROUSED
A KEENER INTEREST, FOR THE APE-MAN WAS
JUST COMMENCING TO ASK HIMSELF
QUESTIONS ABOUT ALL THE MYRIAD
WONDERS WHICH HERETOFORE HE
HAD BUT TAKEN FOR GRANTED.

WHAT MADE THE
FLOWER OPEN?

WHAT MADE IT GROW
FROM A TINY BUD TO A
FULL-BLOWN BLOOM?

WHY WAS HE?

WHERE DID NUMA,
THE LION,
COME FROM?

WHO
PLANTED
THE FIRST
TREE?

HOW DID GORO
GET WAY UP IN THE
NIGHT SKY TO CAST
HIS WELCOME LIGHT
UPON THE FEARSOME NOCTURNAL
JUNGLE? AND THE SUN! DID THE
SUN MERELY HAPPEN THERE?

WHY WERE ALL THE PEOPLES OF THE JUNGLE NOT TREES?
WHY WERE THE TREES NOT SOMETHING ELSE? WHY WAS
TARZAN DIFFERENT FROM TAUG, AND TAUG DIFFERENT FROM
BARA, THE DEER, AND BARA DIFFERENT FROM SHEETA, THE
PANTHER, AND WHY WAS NOT SHEETA LIKE
BUTO, THE RHINOCEROS?

WHERE AND HOW, ANYWAY, DID THEY ALL
COME FROM -- THE TREES, THE FLOWERS,
THE INSECTS, THE COUNTLESS
CREATURES OF THE JUNGLE?

QUITE UNEXPECTEDLY, AN IDEA POPPED INTO TARZAN'S HEAD. IN FOLLOWING OUT
THE MANY RAMIFICATIONS OF THE DICTIONARY DEFINITION OF G O D HE HAD COME
UPON THE WORD C R E A T E -- "TO CAUSE TO COME INTO EXISTENCE; TO FORM OUT OF NOTHING."

TARZAN ALMOST HAD ARRIVED AT SOMETHING TANGIBLE WHEN
A DISTANT WAIL STARTLED HIM INTO SENSIBILITY OF THE
PRESENT AND THE REAL. HE RECOGNIZED IT AT ONCE
AS THE VOICE OF GAZAN, TEEKA'S BABY.

THE WAIL WAS IMMEDIATELY
FOLLOWED BY A REAL SCREAM
OF TERROR. LIKE AN ARROW FROM A
BOW, TARZAN SHOT THROUGH THE TREES. AHEAD OF
HIM HE HEARD THE SAVAGE SNARLING OF AN ADULT SHE-APE.
IT WAS TEEKA. THE DANGER MUST BE VERY REAL.

FROM ALL DIRECTIONS THE APES OF KERCHAK WERE HURRYING IN RESPONSE TO THE APPEAL OF THE BALU
AND ITS MOTHER, AND AS THEY CAME, THEIR ROARS REVERBERATED THROUGH THE FOREST.

BUT TARZAN, SWIFTER THAN HIS FELLOWS, DISTANCED THEM ALL. IT WAS HE WHO FIRST BURST UPON THE SCENE. WHAT HE SAW SENT A COLD CHILL THROUGH HIM, FOR THE ENEMY WAS THE MOST LOATHED OF ALL THE JUNGLE CREATURES. IT WAS HISTAH, THE SNAKE--HUGE, PONDEROUS, SLIMY--- AND IN THE FOLDS OF ITS DEADLY EMBRACE WAS TEEKA'S LITTLE BALU, GAZAN.

NOTHING IN THE JUNGLE INSPIRED IN TARZAN SO NEAR A RESEMBLANCE TO FEAR AS DID THE HIDEOUS HISTAH. THE APES, TOO, LOATHED THE TERRIFYING REPTILE AND OF ALL THEIR ENEMIES THERE WAS NONE THEY GAVE A WIDER BERTH THAN HISTAH, THE SNAKE.

TEEKA WAS
PARTICULARLY
FEARFUL OF THIS
SILENT, REPULSIVE FOE,
AND IT WAS HER ACTION
WHICH FILLED TARZAN
WITH THE GREATEST
WONDER.

FOR AT THE MOMENT THAT
HE SAW HER, THE SHE-APE LEAPED
UPON THE GLISTENING
BODY OF THE SNAKE.

NOR WAS TEEKA'S INNATE DREAD OF THE
MONSTER MUCH GREATER THAN TARZAN'S OWN.
NEVER, WILLINGLY, HAD HE TOUCHED A SNAKE.
YET TARZAN DID NOT HESITATE MORE THAN HAD TEEKA,
BUT LEAPED UPON HISTAH WITH ALL THE SPEED AND
IMPETUOSITY THAT HE WOULD HAVE SHOWN HAD
HE BEEN SPRINGING UPON BARA, THE DEER.

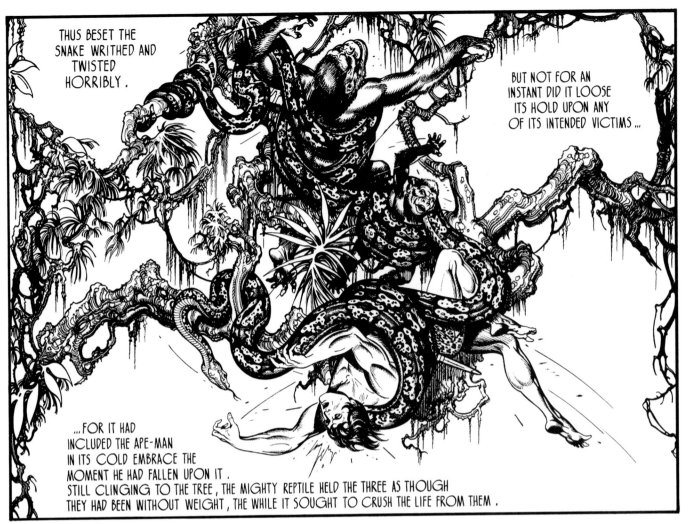

THUS BESET THE SNAKE WRITHED AND TWISTED HORRIBLY .

BUT NOT FOR AN INSTANT DID IT LOOSE ITS HOLD UPON ANY OF ITS INTENDED VICTIMS ...

...FOR IT HAD INCLUDED THE APE-MAN IN ITS COLD EMBRACE THE MOMENT HE HAD FALLEN UPON IT . STILL CLINGING TO THE TREE , THE MIGHTY REPTILE HELD THE THREE AS THOUGH THEY HAD BEEN WITHOUT WEIGHT , THE WHILE IT SOUGHT TO CRUSH THE LIFE FROM THEM .

TARZAN HAD DRAWN HIS KNIFE AND THIS HE NOW PLUNGED RAPIDLY INTO THE BODY OF HIS ENEMY .

BUT THE ENCIRCLING FOLDS PROMISED TO SAP HIS STRENGTH BEFORE HE HAD INFLICTED A DEATH WOUND ON THE SNAKE . YET AS HE FOUGHT AGAINST THE HORRID DEATH THAT CONFRONTED HIM -- HIS SOLE AIM WAS TO SLAY HISTAH AND FREE TEEKA AND HER BALU .

THE GREAT, WIDE-GAPING JAWS OF THE SNAKE TURNED AND HOVERED ABOVE HIM. HISTAH, IN TURNING HIS ATTENTION UPON THE APE-MAN, BROUGHT HIS HEAD WITHIN REACH OF TARZAN'S BLADE.

INSTANTLY A BROWN HAND LEAPED FORWARD AND SEIZED THE MOTTLED NECK ...

... AND ANOTHER DROVE THE HEAVY HUNTING KNIFE TO THE HILT INTO THE REPTILE'S BRAIN.

CONVULSIVELY HISTAH SHUDDERED AND TENSED ...

...WHIPPING AND STRIKING WITH HIS GREAT BODY. HISTAH WAS DYING, BUT IN HIS DEATH THROES HE MIGHT EASILY DISPATCH A DOZEN APES OR MEN. QUICKLY TARZAN SEIZED TEEKA, DRAGGED HER FROM THE LOOSENED EMBRACE, AND DROPPED HER TO THE GROUND.

THEN HE EXTRICATED THE BALU AND TOSSED IT TO ITS MOTHER.

STILL HISTAH WHIPPED ABOUT, CLINGING TO THE APE-MAN. NOW TARZAN WRIGGLED FREE AND LEAPED AWAY OUT OF RANGE OF THE MIGHTY BATTERING OF THE DYING SNAKE.

A CIRCLE OF APES SURROUNDED THE
SCENE OF THE BATTLE; BUT THE MOMENT TARZAN
BROKE SAFELY FROM THE ENEMY, THEY TURNED AWAY TO RESUME
THEIR FEEDING. THE BATTLE OVER, TARZAN WAS EQUALLY INDIFFERENT AND MERELY CAST A PARTING
GLANCE AT THE STILL WRITHING BODY OF HISTAH. HE WANDERED OFF TOWARD THE POOL WHICH SERVED TO WATER THE TRIBE.

STRANGELY, HE DID NOT GIVE
THE VICTORY CRY OVER THE
VANQUISHED HISTAH. WHY, HE
COULD NOT HAVE TOLD YOU,
OTHER THAN TO HIM HISTAH WAS NOT AN ANIMAL. HE DIFFERED
IN SOME PECULIAR WAY FROM THE OTHER DENIZENS OF THE JUNGLE.

AT THE POOL, TARZAN DRANK HIS FILL AND LAY STRETCHED OUT IN THE SHADE OF A TREE. HIS MIND REVERTED TO THE BATTLE WITH HISTAH.

IT SEEMED STRANGE TO HIM THAT TEEKA SHOULD HAVE LEAPED INTO THE FOLDS OF THE HORRID MONSTER. WHY HAD SHE DONE IT? WHY, INDEED, HAD HE? PRESENTLY IT OCCURRED TO HIM THAT HE HAD ACTED ALMOST INVOLUNTARILY, JUST AS HE HAD ACTED WHEN HE HAD RELEASED THE OLD GOMANGANI THE PREVIOUS EVENING.

WHAT MADE HIM DO SUCH THINGS ? SOMEBODY MORE POWERFUL THAN TARZAN MUST FORCE HIM TO ACT AT TIMES. "ALL-POWERFUL," THOUGHT TARZAN. "IT MUST BE THAT GOD MADE ME DO THESE THINGS. IT WAS GOD WHO MADE TEEKA RUSH UPON HISTAH. IT WAS GOD WHO HELD MY KNIFE FROM THE THROAT OF THE OLD GOMANGANI. GOD ACCOMPLISHES THESE STRANGE THINGS FOR HE IS 'ALL-POWERFUL'. I CANNOT SEE HIM ; BUT I KNOW GOD DOES THESE THINGS. NO MANGANI, NO GOMANGANI, NO TARMANGANI COULD DO THEM."

AND WHAT WAS GOD?

OF THAT TARZAN HAD NO
CONCEPTION; BUT HE WAS
SURE THAT EVERYTHING GOOD
CAME FROM GOD. HIS GOOD
ACT IN REFRAINING FROM
SLAYING THE DEFENSELESS OLD
GOMANGANI; TEEKA'S LOVE
THAT HAD HURLED HER INTO THE
EMBRACE OF DEATH; HIS OWN
LOYALTY TO TEEKA, WHICH HAD
JEOPARDIZED HIS LIFE THAT SHE MIGHT
LIVE. THE GOOD AND BEAUTIFUL
TREES AND FLOWERS,
GOD HAD MADE THEM.

HE MADE THE OTHER CREATURES, TOO, THAT EACH MIGHT HAVE FOOD UPON WHICH TO LIVE.

HE HAD MADE SHEETA, THE PANTHER, WITH HIS BEAUTIFUL COAT; AND NUMA, THE LION, WITH HIS NOBLE HEAD AND SHAGGY MANE. HE HAD MADE BARA, THE DEER, LOVELY AND GRACEFUL.

YES, TARZAN HAD FOUND GOD, AND
HE SPENT THE WHOLE DAY IN ATTRIBUTING
TO HIM ALL OF THE GOOD AND BEAUTIFUL
THINGS OF NATURE; BUT THERE WAS ONE
THING WHICH TROUBLED HIM. HE
COULD NOT QUITE RECONCILE
IT TO HIS CONCEPTION OF
HIS NEW-FOUND GOD.

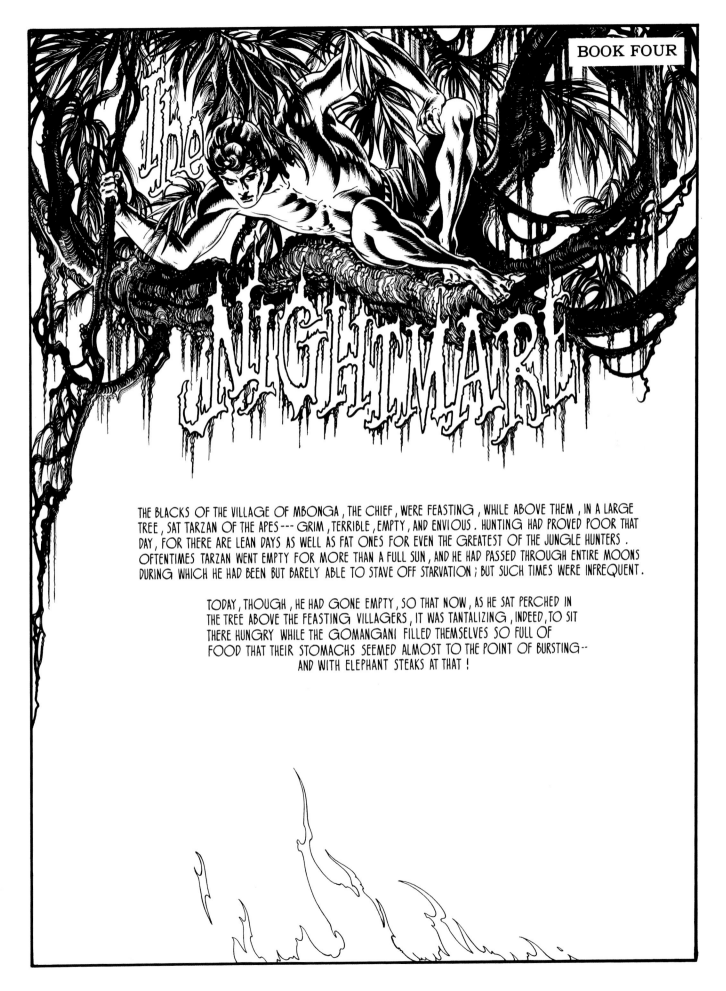

BOOK FOUR

THE NIGHTMARE

THE BLACKS OF THE VILLAGE OF MBONGA, THE CHIEF, WERE FEASTING, WHILE ABOVE THEM, IN A LARGE TREE, SAT TARZAN OF THE APES --- GRIM, TERRIBLE, EMPTY, AND ENVIOUS. HUNTING HAD PROVED POOR THAT DAY, FOR THERE ARE LEAN DAYS AS WELL AS FAT ONES FOR EVEN THE GREATEST OF THE JUNGLE HUNTERS. OFTENTIMES TARZAN WENT EMPTY FOR MORE THAN A FULL SUN, AND HE HAD PASSED THROUGH ENTIRE MOONS DURING WHICH HE HAD BEEN BUT BARELY ABLE TO STAVE OFF STARVATION; BUT SUCH TIMES WERE INFREQUENT.

TODAY, THOUGH, HE HAD GONE EMPTY, SO THAT NOW, AS HE SAT PERCHED IN THE TREE ABOVE THE FEASTING VILLAGERS, IT WAS TANTALIZING, INDEED, TO SIT THERE HUNGRY WHILE THE GOMANGANI FILLED THEMSELVES SO FULL OF FOOD THAT THEIR STOMACHS SEEMED ALMOST TO THE POINT OF BURSTING -- AND WITH ELEPHANT STEAKS AT THAT!

IT WAS WELL PAST MIDNIGHT BEFORE TARZAN EVEN COULD BEGIN TO SEE THE END OF THE ORGY. THE BLACKS WERE FALLING ASLEEP; BUT A FEW STILL PERSISTED

WITH EVIDENCES OF GREAT DISCOMFORT, HE WOULD CRAWL TOWARD THE POT AND REACH INTO THE RECEPT-ACLE TO SEIZE A PIECE OF MEAT. THEN, WITH A GROAN, HE WOULD SLOWLY FORCE THE MORSEL DOWN INTO HIS GORGED STOMACH.

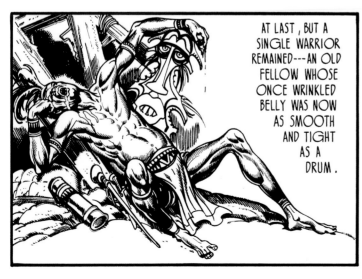

AT LAST, BUT A SINGLE WARRIOR REMAINED---AN OLD FELLOW WHOSE ONCE WRINKLED BELLY WAS NOW AS SMOOTH AND TIGHT AS A DRUM.

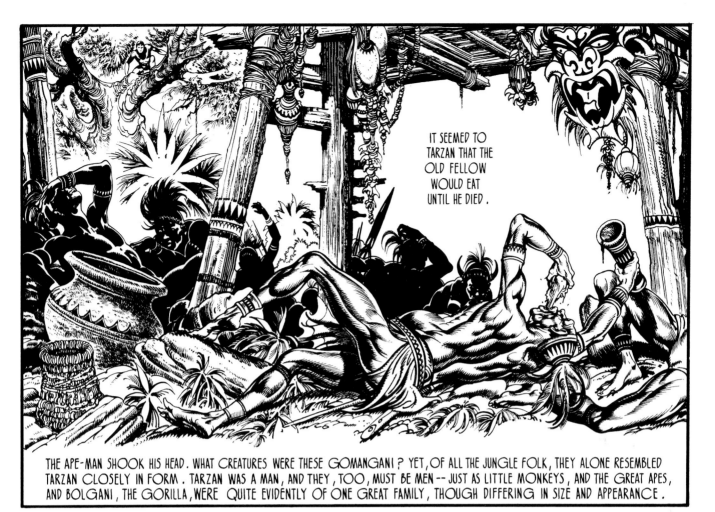

IT SEEMED TO TARZAN THAT THE OLD FELLOW WOULD EAT UNTIL HE DIED.

THE APE-MAN SHOOK HIS HEAD. WHAT CREATURES WERE THESE GOMANGANI? YET, OF ALL THE JUNGLE FOLK, THEY ALONE RESEMBLED TARZAN CLOSELY IN FORM. TARZAN WAS A MAN, AND THEY, TOO, MUST BE MEN -- JUST AS LITTLE MONKEYS, AND THE GREAT APES, AND BOLGANI, THE GORILLA, WERE QUITE EVIDENTLY OF ONE GREAT FAMILY, THOUGH DIFFERING IN SIZE AND APPEARANCE.

TARZAN WAS ASHAMED, FOR OF ALL THE BEASTS OF THE JUNGLE, IT SEEMED TO HIM THEN THAT MAN WAS THE MOST DETESTABLE -- MAN AND DANGO, THE HYENA.

TARZAN COULD ENDURE HIS HUNGER NO LONGER. SILENTLY HE SLIPPED TO THE GROUND WITH THE BOLE OF THE GREAT TREE BETWEEN HIMSELF AND THE FEASTER.

STEALTHILY TARZAN EASED TOWARD THE COOKING POT; AND FORTUNATELY, THAT WAS PRECISELY THE MOMENT THE OLD ONE CHOSE TO SETTLE INTO A STUPOR.

TARZAN SCOOPED SEVERAL PIECES OF MEAT FROM THE POT -- ENOUGH TO SATISFY HIS GREAT HUNGER.

THEN HE PICKED UP A VESSEL CONTAINING BEER ...

... BUT AT THE FIRST TASTE HE SPAT THE STUFF FROM HIS MOUTH. HE WAS SURE EVEN DANGO WOULD DRAW THE LINE AT SUCH A FILTHY TASTING DRINK AS THAT.

TARZAN SWUNG OFF INTO THE JUNGLE
SOME DISTANCE AWAY BEFORE HE PAUSED TO
PARTAKE OF HIS STOLEN FOOD.

HE NOTICED THAT IT GAVE FORTH A STRANGE AND UN-
PLEASANT ODOR, BUT ASSUMED THAT THIS WAS DUE TO THE
FACT THAT IT HAD STOOD IN A VESSEL ABOVE A FIRE.
TARZAN WAS, OF COURSE, UNACCUS-
TOMED TO COOKED FOOD.

HE DID NOT LIKE IT; BUT HE WAS VERY HUNGRY AND HAD EATEN
A CONSIDERABLE PORTION OF HIS HAUL BEFORE IT WAS
REALLY BORNE UPON HIM THAT THE STUFF WAS NAUSEATING.
IT REQUIRED FAR LESS THAN HE HAD IMAGINED
TO SATISFY HIS APPETITE.

THROWING THE BALANCE TO THE GROUND, HE CURLED
UP IN A CONVENIENT CROTCH AND SOUGHT SLUMBER;
BUT SLUMBER SEEMED DIFFICULT TO WOO. ORDINARILY
TARZAN OF THE APES WAS ASLEEP QUICKLY, BUT TONIGHT
HE SQUIRMED AND TWISTED.

AT THE PIT OF HIS STOMACH
WAS A PECULIAR FEELING THAT
RESEMBLED AN ATTEMPT UPON THE
PART OF THE FRAGMENTS OF ELEPHANT
MEAT REPOSING THERE TO COME OUT INTO
THE NIGHT AND SEARCH FOR THEIR ELEPHANT.

BUT TARZAN WAS ADAMANT. HE
GRITTED HIS TEETH AND HELD THEM
BACK. HE WAS NOT TO BE ROBBED
OF HIS MEAL AFTER WAITING SO
LONG TO OBTAIN IT.

HE HAD SUCCEEDED IN DOZING WHEN THE ROARING OF A LION AWOKE HIM. HE SAT UP TO DISCOVER THAT IT WAS BROAD DAYLIGHT.

TARZAN RUBBED HIS EYES. COULD IT BE THAT HE HAD REALLY SLEPT? HE DID NOT FEEL PARTICULARLY REFRESHED AS HE SHOULD HAVE AFTER A GOOD SLEEP.

A NOISE ATTRACTED HIS ATTENTION, AND HE LOOKED DOWN TO SEE A LION STANDING AT THE FOOT OF THE TREE GAZING HUNGRILY AT HIM.

NOW, NEVER BEFORE HAD TARZAN SEEN A LION CLIMB A TREE ...

TARZAN MADE A FACE AT THE KING OF BEASTS, WHEREAT NUMA, GREATLY TO THE APE-MAN'S FASCINATION, STARTED TO CLIMB UP INTO THE BRANCHES TOWARD HIM.

...YET, FOR SOME UNACCOUNTABLE REASON, HE WAS NOT GREATLY SURPRISED THAT THIS PARTICULAR LION SHOULD DO SO.

AS THE LION CLIMBED SLOWLY TOWARD HIM, TARZAN SOUGHT HIGHER BRANCHES. HE COULD SEE THE HUNGRY LIGHT IN THE YELLOW-GREEN EYES.

HE COULD SEE THE SLAVER ON THE DROOPING JOWLS, AND THE GREAT FANGS AGAPE TO SEIZE AND DESTROY HIM. DESPERATELY, HE REACHED THE MORE SLENDER BRANCHES WHERE HE WELL KNEW NO LION COULD FOLLOW; YET ON AND ON CAME DEVIL-FACED NUMA.

AT LAST TARZAN STOOD BALANCED UPON THE VERY PINNACLE OF A SWAYING BRANCH, HIGH ABOVE THE FOREST. HE COULD GO NO FARTHER.

BELOW HIM THE LION CAME STEADILY UPWARD...

...AND TARZAN OF THE APES REALIZED THAT AT LAST THE END HAD COME.

HE COULD NOT DO BATTLE UPON A TINY BRANCH WITH NUMA, THE LION, ESPECIALLY WITH SUCH A NUMA!

NEARER AND NEARER CAME THE LION. ANOTHER MOMENT AND HE COULD REACH UP WITH ONE GREAT PAW AND DRAG THE APE-MAN DOWNWARD TO THOSE AWFUL JAWS.

AS NUMA CLOSED IN, A WHIRRING NOISE ABOVE HIS HEAD ...

...CAUSED TARZAN TO GLANCE APPREHENSIVELY UPWARD. A GREAT BIRD WAS CIRCLING CLOSE ABOVE HIM.

THE LION WAS ALREADY REACHING FORTH A TALONED PAW TO SEIZE HIM WHEN THE BIRD SWOOPED ...

...AND BURIED NO LESS FORMIDABLE TALONS IN TARZAN'S BACK. THE PAIN WAS NUMBING; BUT IT WAS WITH A SENSE OF RELIEF THAT THE APE-MAN FELT HIMSELF SNATCHED FROM THE CLUTCHES OF NUMA.

WITH A GREAT WHIRRING OF WINGS, THE BIRD ROSE
RAPIDLY UNTIL THE FOREST LAY FAR BELOW. IT MADE TARZAN
SICK AND DIZZY TO LOOK DOWN UPON IT FROM SO GREAT A HEIGHT, SO HE CLOSED HIS EYES TIGHT
AND HELD HIS BREATH. HIGHER AND HIGHER CLIMBED THE HUGE BIRD. TARZAN OPENED HIS EYES. THE JUNGLE WAS
SO FAR AWAY THAT HE COULD SEE ONLY A DIM, GREEN BLUR BELOW HIM.

THEN A SUDDEN
MADNESS SEIZED HIM.
WHERE WAS THE BIRD TAKING
HIM? WAS HE TO SUBMIT THUS
PASSIVELY TO A FEATHERED CREATURE
HOWEVER ENORMOUS? WAS HE, TARZAN OF THE APES,
MIGHTY FIGHTER, TO DIE WITHOUT STRIKING A BLOW IN HIS OWN DEFENSE? NEVER!

HE SEIZED THE HUNTING BLADE AND THRUSTING UPWARD DROVE IT ONCE, TWICE, THRICE INTO THE BREAST ABOVE HIM. THE MIGHTY WINGS FLUTTERED A FEW MORE TIMES, SPASMODICALLY, THE TALONS RELEASED THEIR HOLD, AND TARZAN OF THE APES FELL HURTLING DOWNWARD TOWARD THE DISTANT JUNGLE.

IT SEEMED TO THE APE-MAN THAT HE FELL FOR MANY MINUTES BEFORE HE CRASHED THROUGH THE LEAFY VERDURE OF THE TREE TOPS.

THE SMALLER BRANCHES BROKE HIS FALL ...

... SO THAT HE CAME TO REST FOR AN INSTANT UPON THE VERY BRANCH UPON WHICH HE HAD SOUGHT SLUMBER THE PREVIOUS NIGHT.

ONCE MORE HE
OPENED HIS EYES,
WHICH HE HAD
CLOSED DURING
THE FALL. AGAIN
IT WAS
NIGHT.

BELOW HIM A LION ROARED, AND, LOOKING
DOWNWARD, TARZAN COULD SEE THE YELLOW-
GREEN EYES SHINING AS THEY BORED HUNGRILY
UPWARD THROUGH THE DARKNESS TOWARD HIM.

THE APE-MAN GASPED FOR BREATH. COLD SWEAT STOOD
OUT FROM EVERY PORE; THERE WAS A GREAT SICKNESS
AT THE PIT OF TARZAN'S STOMACH. TARZAN OF THE APES
HAD DREAMED HIS FIRST DREAM.

FOR A LONG TIME HE SAT WATCHING FOR
NUMA TO CLIMB INTO THE TREE AFTER HIM,
AND LISTENING FOR THE SOUND OF THE
GREAT WINGS FROM ABOVE, FOR TO TARZAN
OF THE APES HIS DREAM WAS A REALITY.

HE COULD NOT BELIEVE
WHAT HE HAD SEEN AND YET, HAVING
SEEN EVEN THESE INCREDIBLE THINGS, HE COULD
NOT DISBELIEVE THE EVIDENCE OF HIS OWN PER-
CEPTIONS. NEVER IN ALL HIS LIFE HAD TARZAN'S SENSES
DECEIVED HIM BADLY, AND SO, NATURALLY, HE HAD GREAT
FAITH IN THEM. EACH PERCEPTION WHICH EVER HAD BEEN
TRANSMITTED TO TARZAN'S BRAIN HAD BEEN, WITH VARYING
ACCURACY, A TRUE PERCEPTION. HE COULD NOT CONCEIVE
OF THE POSSIBILITY OF APPARENTLY HAVING PASSED THROUGH
SUCH A WEIRD ADVENTURE IN WHICH THERE WAS NO GRAIN OF TRUTH.
YET HE KNEW THAT NUMA COULD NOT CLIMB A TREE, HE KNEW THAT
THERE EXISTED IN THE JUNGLE NO SUCH BIRD AS HE HAD SEEN, AND HE
KNEW, TOO, THAT HE COULD NOT HAVE FALLEN A TINY FRACTION OF THE
DISTANCE HE HAD HURTLED DOWNWARD, AND LIVED.

AS HE THOUGHT DEEPLY UPON THE STRANGE OCCURRENCES OF THE NIGHT, HE WITNESSED ANOTHER REMARKABLE HAPPENING. IT WAS INDEED QUITE PREPOSTEROUS, YET HE SAW IT ALL WITH HIS OWN EYES. IT WAS NOTHING LESS THAN HISTAH, THE SNAKE, WINDING HIS SINUOUS WAY UP THE BOLE OF THE TREE BELOW HIM — HISTAH, WITH THE HEAD OF THE OLD MAN OF THE COOKING POT.

AS THE FRIGHTFUL FACE CAME CLOSE TO TARZAN, THE JAWS OPENED TO SEIZE HIM. THE APE-MAN RAISED HIS WEAPON TO STRIKE AT THE HIDEOUS FACE ...

AS THE APE-MAN STRUCK FURIOUSLY, THE APPARITION DISAPPEARED.

TARZAN SAT UPON HIS BRANCH, TREMBLING IN EVERY LIMB, WIDE-EYED AND PANTING. HE LOOKED ALL AROUND HIM BUT HE SAW NAUGHT OF THE OLD MAN WITH THE BODY OF HISTAH.

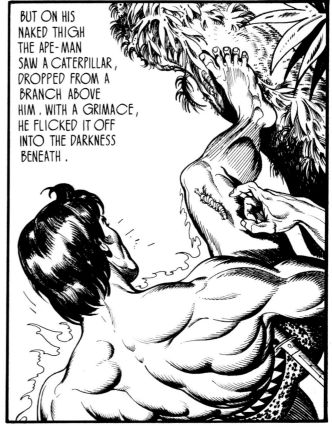

BUT ON HIS NAKED THIGH THE APE-MAN SAW A CATERPILLAR, DROPPED FROM A BRANCH ABOVE HIM. WITH A GRIMACE, HE FLICKED IT OFF INTO THE DARKNESS BENEATH.

AND SO THE NIGHT WORE ON, DREAM FOLLOWING DREAM, NIGHTMARE FOLLOWING NIGHTMARE, UNTIL THE DISTRACTED APE-MAN STARTED LIKE A FRIGHTENED DEER AT THE RUSTLING OF THE WIND IN THE TREES ABOUT HIM, OR LEAPED TO HIS FEET AS THE UNCANNY LAUGH OF A HYENA BURST SUDDENLY UPON A MOMENTARY JUNGLE SILENCE.

BUT AT LAST THE TARDY MORNING BROKE AND A SICK AND FEVERISH TARZAN CAME DOWN SLUGGISHLY INTO THE GLOOMY MAZES OF THE FOREST TO SEARCH FOR WATER.

HIS WHOLE BODY SEEMED ON FIRE, A GREAT SICKNESS SURGED UPWARD TO HIS THROAT.

HE SAW A TANGLE OF ALMOST IMPENETRABLE THICKET, AND, LIKE THE WILD BEAST HE WAS, HE CRAWLED INTO IT TO DIE ALONE AND UNSEEN, SAFE FROM THE ATTACKS OF PREDATORY CARNIVORES.

BUT HE DID NOT DIE. FOR A LONG TIME HE WANTED TO;
BUT PRESENTLY NATURE AND AN OUTRAGED STOMACH RELIEVED
THEMSELVES IN THEIR OWN THERAPEUTIC MANNER; THE APE-MAN BROKE
INTO A VIOLENT PERSPIRATION AND THEN FELL INTO A NORMAL AND UNTROUBLED
SLEEP WHICH PERSISTED WELL INTO THE AFTERNOON. WHEN HE AWOKE, HE FOUND
HIMSELF WEAK BUT NO LONGER SICK. ONCE MORE HE SOUGHT WATER ...

... AND AFTER DRINKING DEEPLY, TOOK
HIS WAY SLOWLY TOWARD THE CABIN BY THE SEA.
IN TIMES OF LONELINESS AND TROUBLE, IT HAD LONG
BEEN HIS CUSTOM TO SEEK THERE THE QUIET AND RESTFULNESS
WHICH HE COULD FIND NOWHERE ELSE.

AS TARZAN ENTERED THE CABIN, TWO SMALL, BLOODSHOT EYES
WATCHED HIM FROM THE CONCEALING FOLIAGE OF THE JUNGLE CLOSE BY.

HERE HE COULD CURL UP AND LOOK AT
THE PICTURES IN THE STRANGE
THINGS WHICH WERE BOOKS.

HE COULD PUZZLE OUT
THE PRINTED WORDS
HE HAD LEARNED
TO READ WITHOUT
KNOWLEDGE OF THE
SPOKEN LANGUAGE
THESE REPRESENTED.
HE COULD LIVE IN
A WONDERFUL
WORLD OF WHICH
HE HAD NO KNOWLEDGE
BEYOND THE COVERS
OF HIS BELOVED
BOOKS.

NUMA AND SABOR MIGHT PROWL ABOUT CLOSE TO HIM, THE
ELEMENTS MIGHT RAGE IN ALL THEIR FURY; BUT HERE AT LEAST,
TARZAN MIGHT BE ENTIRELY OFF HIS GUARD IN A DELIGHTFUL
RELAXATION WHICH GAVE HIM ALL HIS FACULTIES FOR THE
UNINTERRUPTED PURSUIT OF THIS
GREATEST OF ALL HIS PLEASURES.

TODAY HE LOOKED
AT A PICTURE OF A
HUGE BIRD WITH A LITTLE
TARMANGANI IN ITS TALONS. TARZAN FROWNED.
YES, THIS WAS THE VERY BIRD WHICH HAD CARRIED
HIM OFF THE DAY BEFORE.

AND HERE WAS A PICTURE OF NUMA. IT WAS ALL VERY
STRANGE. HE WAS NOW NOT SURE WHERE THE REAL
CEASED AND THE UNREAL BEGAN. HAD HE EATEN
OF ELEPHANT MEAT? HAD HE BEEN SICK?
HAD HE SEEN HISTAH, THE SNAKE?

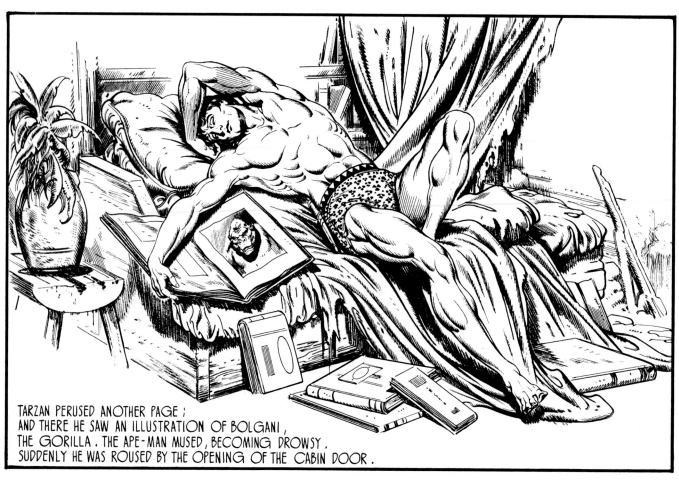

TARZAN PERUSED ANOTHER PAGE;
AND THERE HE SAW AN ILLUSTRATION OF BOLGANI,
THE GORILLA. THE APE-MAN MUSED, BECOMING DROWSY.
SUDDENLY HE WAS ROUSED BY THE OPENING OF THE CABIN DOOR.

TURNING, TARZAN WAS AMAZED TO SEE THE HUGE FORM OF BOLGANI, THE GORILLA. TARZAN NOTED THE JUNGLE MADNESS WHICH SEIZES THE FIERCER MALES WAS UPON BOLGANI. HE REACHED FOR HIS HUNTING KNIFE.

THEN HIS EYES FELL ON THE OPEN PAGE WITH THE PICTURE OF BOLGANI. OF COURSE! HE GRINNED BROADLY AT THE ADVANCING GORILLA.

IN A MOMENT BOLGANI WOULD NO DOUBT TURN INTO PAMBA, THE RAT, WITH THE HEAD OF TANTOR. NO, NOT AGAIN WOULD HE BE FOOLED BY EMPTY THINGS WHICH CAME WHILE HE SLEPT! BUT THIS TIME BOLGANI DID NOT CHANGE. NOW THE THING SHOULD BE FADING AWAY... YET IT DID NOT. THIS WAS QUITE THE MOST REALISTIC OF SLEEP-ADVENTURES, THOUGHT TARZAN, AS HE AMIABLY AWAITED THE NEXT AMUSING INCIDENT.

AND THEN THE GORILLA CHARGED. TWO MIGHTY HANDS SEIZED TARZAN ...

... GREAT FANGS WERE BARED TO HIS FACE, AND A HIDEOUS GROWL FANNED HIS CHEEK.

TARZAN GRINNED AT THE APPARITION. HE KNEW THIS WAS NO REAL BOLGANI. THE GORILLA SEEMED PUZZLED BY THE RELAXED AND PASSIVE ATTITUDE OF THE HAIRLESS APE.

SUDDENLY HE WHIRLED THE APE-MAN TO A SHOULDER AND DASHED OUT INTO THE OPEN, TOWARD THE TREES. NOW INDEED THIS WAS TRULY A SLEEP-ADVENTURE, TARZAN GRINNED.

HE GLANCED BACK AND SAW THE CABIN DOOR WAS WIDE OPEN. THIS WOULD NEVER DO! HE WOULD HAVE TO LATCH IT. HE TRIED TO SLIP FROM BOLGANI'S SHOULDER. BUT THE BEAST GRIPPED HIM TIGHTER.

WITH A MIGHTY EFFORT, THE APE-MAN WRENCHED LOOSE, AND AS HE SLID FREE, THE DREAM GORILLA FEROCIOUSLY BURIED GREAT FANGS IN HIS ARM. THE GRIN FADED FROM TARZAN'S LIPS. ASLEEP OR AWAKE, THIS THING WAS NO LONGER A JOKE!

BITING AND TEARING, THE TWO ROLLED UPON THE GROUND IN FEARSOME BATTLE.

259

TARZAN FOUGHT OFF THE INSANE BEAST, STRAINED TO RISE TO AIM HIS KNIFE AT THE SAVAGE HEART.

IN A QUICK MOVEMENT THE KEEN BLADE PLUNGED TO ITS GOAL. BOLGANI VOICED A SINGLE FRIGHTFUL SHRIEK, STAGGERED, AND PLUNGED TO EARTH.

TARZAN OF THE APES LOOKED DOWN UPON HIS KILL. HE REACHED DOWN AND TOUCHED THE DEAD BODY. THE LIFEBLOOD CRIMSONED HIS FINGERS. RAISING HIS HAND, HE SNIFFED. HE SHOOK HIS HEAD AND TURNED TO THE CABIN.

WHEN HE HAD CLOSED THE LATCH, HE RETURNED TO THE BODY OF HIS KILL.

THE GORILLA HAD NOT DISAPPEARED. HE PLACED A FOOT ON THE PROSTRATE FORM ...

... AND GAVE VOICE TO THE FIERCE CRY OF THE BULL APE.

IT ALL SEEMED VERY REAL NOW; YET HE DID NOT KNOW. PUZZLED, HE TURNED AWAY INTO THE JUNGLE. BUT THERE WAS ONE THING HE DID KNOW. NEVER AGAIN WOULD HE EAT THE FLESH OF TANTOR, THE ELEPHANT.

HOGARTH

EDGAR RICE BURROUGHS'
Tarzan®

Swing into adventure with these thrilling tales of Edgar Rice Burroughs' iconic jungle hero, Tarzan, King of the Apes!

TARZAN: BURNE HOGARTH'S LORD OF THE JUNGLE HC
ISBN 978-1-61655-537-5 | $49.99

EDGAR RICE BURROUGHS' TARZAN: THE SUNDAY COMICS
Volume 1, 1931–1933 HC
ISBN 978-1-61655-117-9 | $125.00
Volume 2, 1933–1935 HC
ISBN 978-1-61655-419-4 | $125.00

TARZAN: THE JESSE MARSH YEARS
Volume 1 HC | ISBN 978-1-59582-238-3 | $49.99
Volume 2 HC | ISBN 978-1-59582-294-9 | $49.99
Volume 3 HC | ISBN 978-1-59582-379-3 | $49.99
Volume 4 HC | ISBN 978-1-59582-392-2 | $49.99
Volume 5 HC | ISBN 978-1-59582-426-4 | $49.99
Volume 6 HC | ISBN 978-1-59582-497-4 | $49.99
Volume 7 HC | ISBN 978-1-59582-547-6 | $49.99
Volume 8 HC | ISBN 978-1-59582-548-3 | $49.99
Volume 9 HC | ISBN 978-1-59582-649-7 | $49.99
Volume 10 HC | ISBN 978-1-59582-753-1 | $49.99
Volume 11 HC | ISBN 978-1-59582-754-8 | $49.99

TARZAN: THE JOE KUBERT YEARS
Volume 1 HC | ISBN 978-1-59307-404-3 | $49.99
Volume 3 HC | ISBN 978-1-59307-417-3 | $49.99

TARZAN: THE RUSS MANNING YEARS
Volume 1 HC | ISBN 978-1-59582-937-5 | $49.99

BATMAN/TARZAN: CLAWS OF THE CAT-WOMAN TPB
ISBN 978-1-56971-466-9 | $10.99

SUPERMAN/TARZAN: SONS OF THE JUNGLE TPB
ISBN 978-1-56971-761-5 | $9.99

TARZAN VS. PREDATOR AT THE EARTH'S CORE TPB
ISBN 978-1-56971-231-3 | $12.99

EDGAR RICE BURROUGHS' TARZAN THE UNTAMED TPB
ISBN 978-1-56971-418-8 | $11.99

TARZAN: CARSON OF VENUS TPB
ISBN 978-1-56971-379-2 | $12.99

TARZAN: LE MONSTRE TPB
ISBN 978-1-56971-296-2 | $16.99

TARZAN: THE LOST ADVENTURE HC
ISBN 978-1-56971-083-8 | $19.99

TARZAN: THE LOST ADVENTURE LIMITED EDITION HC
ISBN 978-1-56971-128-6 | $99.99

THE UNAUTHORIZED TARZAN HC
ISBN 978-1-61655-070-7 | $29.99

THE UNAUTHORIZED TARZAN LIMITED EDITION HC
ISBN 978-1-61655-094-3 | $59.99